First World War
and Army of Occupation
War Diary
France, Belgium and Germany

61 DIVISION
183 Infantry Brigade
Worcestershire Regiment
2/7th Battalion
2 September 1915 - 18 January 1918

WO95/3060/3

The Naval & Military Press Ltd
www.nmarchive.com
Published in association with The National Archives

Published by

The Naval & Military Press Ltd

Unit 10 Ridgewood Industrial Park,

Uckfield, East Sussex,

TN22 5QE England

Tel: +44 (0) 1825 749494

www.naval-military-press.com

www.nmarchive.com

This diary has been reprinted in facsimile from the original. Any imperfections are inevitably reproduced and the quality may fall short of modern type and cartographic standards.

© Crown Copyright
Images reproduced by permission of The National Archives, London, England, 2015.

Contents

Document type	Place/Title	Date From	Date To
Heading	61st Division 183rd Infy Bde 2-7th Bn Worcs Regt. 1915 Sep-1918 Jan		
Miscellaneous	War Diary Summary 2/7 Bn. Worc. Rgt Maldon.	01/09/1915	01/09/1915
Heading	War Diary Of 2/7. Worcester Regt. From 1.9.15 To 30.9.15		
War Diary	Maldon	02/09/1915	02/09/1915
War Diary	Epping	04/09/1915	30/09/1915
War Diary	Brentwood	04/10/1915	29/11/1915
War Diary	Brentwood	03/11/1915	29/11/1915
Heading	War Diary Of 2/7th. Battalion Worcestershire Regiment From 1st. December 1915 To 31st. December 1915		
War Diary	Brentwood	01/12/1915	31/12/1915
Heading	War Diary Of 2/7th Battalion The Worcestershire Regiment. From 1st January, 1916, To 31st January, 1916.		
War Diary	Brentwood	01/01/1916	31/01/1916
Miscellaneous	Tactical Exercise 27th January, 1916 2/7th Battalion Worcestershire Regiment. Operation Orders By Colonel A. G. Peyton.		
Miscellaneous	Operation Orders By Colonel A. G. Peyton Commanding 2/7th Worcester Regt.	26/01/1916	26/01/1916
War Diary	Brentwood		
Miscellaneous	Tactical Exercise 14th January, 1916. 183rd Brigade. Operation Orders By Brigadier General Sir John Barnsley V. D. Appendix "A"		
Miscellaneous	Tactical Exercise On Jan 14/16.	10/01/1916	10/01/1916
Operation(al) Order(s)	Operation Order No. 37. By Col. Sir John Barnsley V. D. Commanding 183rd. Infantry Brigade.	11/01/1916	11/01/1916
Miscellaneous	Operation Orders By Captain E H Grainger Commanding 2/7th Worcester Regt	12/01/1916	12/01/1916
Heading	War Diary Of 2/7th Bn The Worcestershire Regiment From 23rd May 1916 To 31st May 1916. Volume 1		
War Diary	Tidworth	23/05/1916	23/05/1916
War Diary	Southampton	24/05/1916	24/05/1916
War Diary	Havre	25/05/1916	26/05/1916
War Diary	Robecq	27/05/1916	30/05/1916
War Diary	Vieille Chappelle	31/05/1916	10/06/1916
War Diary	Pont Du Hem	11/06/1916	15/06/1916
War Diary	Neuve Chapelle	16/06/1916	21/06/1916
War Diary	La Gorgue	22/06/1916	30/06/1916
Heading	War Diary Of 2/7th Bn Worcestershire Regt. From 1st. July 1916 To 31st July 1916 Vol 3.		
War Diary	La Gorgue	01/07/1916	02/07/1916
War Diary	Fauquissart Right Sector	03/07/1916	10/07/1916
War Diary	Laventie	11/07/1916	18/07/1916
War Diary	Fauquissart Left Sector	19/07/1916	31/07/1916
War Diary	Awarded	28/07/1916	06/09/1916
Heading	War Diary Of 7th Battn The Worcestershire Regt. Aug 1st 31st 1916 Vol 4		
War Diary	Laventie	01/08/1916	01/08/1916

War Diary	Fauquissant	02/08/1916	05/08/1916
War Diary	Laventie	06/08/1916	08/08/1916
War Diary	Le Grand Pacaut	09/08/1916	17/08/1916
War Diary	Neuvechapelle	18/08/1916	21/08/1916
War Diary	Croix Barbee	22/08/1916	31/08/1916
Heading	183rd Infantry Brigade War Diary Of 2/7th Worcester Regiment For September 1916		
War Diary	Moated Grange	01/09/1916	01/09/1916
War Diary	Riez Bailleul	02/09/1916	06/09/1916
War Diary	Moated Grange	07/09/1916	10/09/1916
War Diary	La Gorcue	11/09/1916	16/09/1916
War Diary	Neuve Chapelle	17/09/1916	20/09/1916
War Diary	La Fosse	21/09/1916	25/09/1916
War Diary	Neuve Chapelle	26/09/1916	30/09/1916
Heading	183 Inf Bde. 2/7th Worcestershire Regt. War Diary For October 1916 Vol 6		
War Diary	Neuve Chapelle	01/10/1916	01/10/1916
War Diary	La Fosse	02/10/1916	07/10/1916
War Diary	Neuve Chapelle	08/10/1916	13/10/1916
War Diary	Croix Barbee	14/10/1916	19/10/1916
War Diary	Neuve Chapelle	20/10/1916	24/10/1916
War Diary	Croix Barbee	25/10/1916	26/10/1916
War Diary	L'Eclair	27/10/1916	31/10/1916
Heading	War Diary Of 2/7th Battn The Worcestershire Regt For November 1916		
War Diary	L'Ecleme To Cauchy-Area Tour	01/11/1916	01/11/1916
War Diary	Marquay	02/11/1916	02/11/1916
War Diary	Villers Brulin	03/11/1916	04/11/1916
War Diary	Mont-En-Ternois	05/11/1916	05/11/1916
War Diary	Noeux	06/11/1916	14/11/1916
War Diary	Autheau	15/11/1916	15/11/1916
War Diary	Stouen	16/11/1916	16/11/1916
War Diary	Near St Pierre Divion	17/11/1916	20/11/1916
War Diary	Aveluy	21/11/1916	21/11/1916
War Diary	Ovillers	22/11/1916	25/11/1916
War Diary	Nr Aveluy	26/11/1916	29/11/1916
War Diary	Nr Ovillers	30/11/1916	30/11/1916
Heading	War Diary. 2/7 Worcesters. December 1916.		
War Diary	Ovillers	01/12/1916	04/12/1916
War Diary	Mouquetfarn	05/12/1916	09/12/1916
War Diary	Nr Martinsart	10/12/1916	11/12/1916
War Diary	Hedauville	12/12/1916	21/12/1916
War Diary	Nr Martinsart	22/12/1916	27/12/1916
War Diary	Mouquet Farm Right Sector	28/12/1916	31/12/1916
Heading	War Diary Of 2/7th. Battn. The Worcestershire Regt. From 1st. To 31st. January 1917		
War Diary	Mouquet Farm Re Sector To Wellington Huts Nabroad	01/01/1917	05/01/1917
War Diary	Martin-Sart	06/01/1917	14/01/1917
War Diary	Narenne	15/01/1917	15/01/1917
War Diary	Varennes Co Beauquesne	16/01/1917	16/01/1917
War Diary	Heuzecourt	17/01/1917	17/01/1917
War Diary	Agenville	18/01/1917	18/01/1917
War Diary	Marcheville	19/01/1917	31/01/1917
Heading	February 1917 War Diary Of 2/7th Worcester Regt.		
War Diary	Marcheville	01/02/1917	03/02/1917
War Diary	Bussus-Bussuel	04/02/1917	13/02/1917

War Diary	Wiencourt	14/02/1917	15/02/1917
War Diary	Framerville	16/02/1917	16/02/1917
War Diary	Chaulnes Section	17/02/1917	24/02/1917
War Diary	Harbonnieres	25/02/1917	28/02/1917
Heading	March 1917 War Diary Of 2/7th Battn The Worcs Regt		
War Diary	Harbonnieres	01/03/1917	07/03/1917
War Diary	Vauvillers	08/03/1917	08/03/1917
War Diary	Chaulnes	09/03/1917	12/03/1917
War Diary	Framerville	13/03/1917	17/03/1917
War Diary	Polygon Wood Nr Chaulnes	18/03/1917	18/03/1917
War Diary	C2sc 1/2.7. Map 66 D. NW.	19/03/1917	24/03/1917
War Diary	C2S.C 1/2.7. Map. 66D.N.W. To Morchain	25/03/1917	27/03/1917
War Diary	Monchy-La Gache	28/03/1917	31/03/1917
Heading	April 1917 War Diary Of 2/7th Worcester Regt.		
War Diary	Villeveque To Marteville	01/04/1917	01/04/1917
War Diary	Villecholes	02/04/1917	03/04/1917
War Diary	Villeveque	04/04/1917	05/04/1917
War Diary	Marteville	06/04/1917	06/04/1917
War Diary	Monchy-La Gache	07/04/1917	08/04/1917
War Diary	Croix Molignaux	09/04/1917	20/04/1917
War Diary	Germaine	21/04/1917	30/04/1917
Heading	May 1917 War Diary Of 2/7th Worcester Regiment		
War Diary	Germaine	01/05/1917	01/05/1917
War Diary	Left Support Holnon Sector	02/05/1917	05/05/1917
War Diary	Out Post Line Holnon Sector	06/05/1917	09/05/1917
War Diary	Attilly	10/05/1917	14/05/1917
War Diary	Germaine	15/05/1917	16/05/1917
War Diary	Herly	17/05/1917	17/05/1917
War Diary	Villers-Bocage	18/05/1917	20/05/1917
War Diary	Behoval	21/05/1917	22/05/1917
War Diary	Susst Leger	23/05/1917	23/05/1917
War Diary	Dainville	24/05/1917	31/05/1917
Heading	War Diary Of 2/7th Battn Worcestershire Regt.		
War Diary	Tilloy	01/06/1917	09/06/1917
War Diary	Simencourt	10/06/1917	30/06/1917
Heading	2/7th Worcesters War Diary July 1917.		
War Diary	Vieil Hesdin	01/07/1917	23/07/1917
War Diary	Flers	24/07/1917	25/07/1917
War Diary	Eringhem	26/07/1917	31/07/1917
Heading	August 1917 War Diary Of 2/7th Bn. The Worcestershire Regt		
War Diary	Eringhem	01/09/1917	14/09/1917
War Diary	Poperinghe	15/08/1917	15/08/1917
War Diary	Ypres	16/08/1917	21/08/1917
War Diary	Wieltje Ypres	22/08/1917	28/08/1917
War Diary	Wieltje	29/08/1917	29/08/1917
War Diary	Vlamertinghe	30/08/1917	31/08/1917
Heading	September 1917 War Diary Of 2/7th Bn The Worcestershire Regt.		
War Diary	Vlamertinge	01/09/1917	07/09/1917
War Diary	Canal Bank	08/09/1917	08/09/1917
War Diary	In The Line E Of Ypres	09/09/1917	14/09/1917
War Diary	Vlamertinge	15/09/1917	15/09/1917
War Diary	Watou	16/09/1917	17/09/1917
War Diary	Wormhoutd	18/09/1917	18/09/1917
War Diary	Arras	19/09/1917	19/09/1917

War Diary	Simencourt	20/09/1917	23/09/1917
War Diary	Arras	24/09/1917	24/09/1917
War Diary	Greenland Hill	25/09/1917	30/09/1917
Heading	October 1917. War Diary Of 2/7th Battn. The Worcestershire Regt Vol 18		
War Diary	Greenland Hill Arras	01/10/1917	04/10/1917
War Diary	St Nicholas Arras	05/10/1917	15/10/1917
War Diary	Fampoux	16/10/1917	31/10/1917
Heading	2/7th Bn. Worcestershire Regt. War Diary Vol 19		
War Diary	Fampoux	01/11/1917	03/11/1917
War Diary	Chemical Works	04/11/1917	09/11/1917
War Diary	Arras	10/11/1917	20/11/1917
War Diary	Greenland Hill	21/11/1917	26/11/1917
War Diary	Green Land Hill Arras	27/11/1917	30/11/1917
Heading	December 1917 War Diary Of 2/7th Bn. The Worcestershire Regt		
War Diary	Trescault	01/12/1917	01/12/1917
War Diary	La Yacquerie Sector	02/12/1917	14/12/1917
War Diary	Villers Pluich	15/12/1917	16/12/1917
War Diary	Havringcourt Wood	17/12/1917	20/12/1917
War Diary	Villers	21/12/1917	21/12/1917
War Diary	Plouch	22/12/1917	22/12/1917
War Diary	Havrincourt Wood	23/12/1917	23/12/1917
War Diary	Etricourt	24/12/1917	24/12/1917
War Diary	Morcourt	25/12/1917	31/12/1917
Miscellaneous	61st Division	03/11/1917	03/11/1917
Miscellaneous	Raid Carried Out By The 2/7th. Battalion The Worcestershire Regiment.	25/10/1917	25/10/1917
Miscellaneous	XVII Corps.	25/10/1917	25/10/1917
Miscellaneous	61st. Division.	25/10/1917	25/10/1917
Miscellaneous	Right Attack.		
Miscellaneous	Not To Be Taken Beyond Battalion H.Q. In The Line. 61st Division Intelligence Summary No. 31.		
Miscellaneous	Annexe To 61st Div. Summary No. 31	25/10/1917	25/10/1917
Miscellaneous	Captain Goodwin's Report.		
Miscellaneous	Capt Goodwin's Raid		
Heading	January 1918 War Diary Of 2/7th Battn. The Worcestershire Regt.		
War Diary	Marcelcave	01/01/1918	07/01/1918
War Diary	Roye	08/01/1918	09/01/1918
War Diary	Buny And Croix	10/01/1918	10/01/1918
War Diary	Moligneaux	11/01/1918	14/01/1918
War Diary	Buny And Croix Moligneaux	15/01/1918	15/01/1918
War Diary	Germaine	16/01/1918	18/01/1918

61ST DIVISION
183RD INFY BDE

2-7TH BN WORCS REGT.

~~MAY 1915 - JAN 1918.~~

1915 SEP - ~~1916 JAN~~

~~1915 MAY~~ - 1918 JAN

(1916 FEB MAR APR DIARIES MISSING)

DISBANDED

War Diary Summary
2/7 B. WORC. Rgt
MALDON.
1.9.15

To O.C. 183 Inf. Bde

August.

Training:- during the month the Bn. dug a section of trenches and practised occupying them for 24 hours, and relieving troops there by day and night. Useful practice was obtained.

Recruits (200) have now joined their companies, and require shooting practice with the full charge on a range –

Transport have now received most of their equipment and require practice in riding and driving and the care and cleaning of harness.

RM Sparkes Lt Col.
2/7 B. Worc Rgt.

Confidential
War Diary
of
2/7. Worcester Regt.
From 1.9.15 *To* 30.9.15

2/7 November Regt

Army Form C. 2118.

WAR DIARY
or
INTELLIGENCE SUMMARY. for September 1915
(Erase heading not required.)

Place	Date	Hour	Summary of Events and Information	Remarks and references to Appendices
MALDON	2.9.15		The Battl. entrained to BRENTWOOD thence to Brigade Camp under Canvas at EPPING.	
EPPING	4.9.15		1 man transferred to 2/Musketiers Corps required for fort work	
-	8."		Do	
-	9."		1 man discharged on medical grounds as not likely to become an efficient soldier	
-	(11.12) 9.15	11.45	1 man discharged on being placed a Communion. 2nd Lieut F.F. FLINT gazetted to the Regt. as 2nd Lieut. There was a Zeppelin raid on the Camps of the 2/6 Leicesters & R.F.A but Bombs were dropped on the Camp of this Battn. No Bombs or Incendiary Bombs were dropped to the Regiment (not yet joined) 2nd Lieut R.M. SMITH gazetted to the Regiment (not yet joined)	
-	13.9.15		4 men discharged on being granted Commissions (They were struck off our strength from 1.6.15, 7.6.15, 2.8.15, 14.9.15 respectively)	
-	14."		1 man taken on strength having been released 5 3/ Leicester Yeomanry Major & Hon: Lt. Col. R.M. DANKS Seconded for duty with a Provisional Battn. (Left Battn 11.9.15)	
-	19."		1 man transferred to 82nd Prov. Battn. having proved to be under age	
-	21."		Do - having been found to be a 17d 1st Class 8 men for Home Service only. 1 man transferred to 2/Monmouths Corps being required for fort work	

Army Form C. 2118.

WAR DIARY
or
INTELLIGENCE SUMMARY. for September 1915
(Erase heading not required.)

Place	Date	Hour	Summary of Events and Information	Remarks and references to Appendices
EPPING	21.9.15		Batt! Band proceeded to Troventurpher to assist in a Recruiting Campaign	
	22.9.15		1 man discharged on being granted a Commission	
	29.9.15		2nd Lieut E.R. CHILDE-FREEMAN posted to the Reft. (not yet joined)	
	30 -		2nd Lieut J.W.D. MELHUISH & 2nd Lieut N. GOUGH struck off the strength on joining the Expeditionary Force.	

Army Form C: 2118.

WAR DIARY
or
INTELLIGENCE SUMMARY. 2/7th Worc. Regt.
(Erase heading not required.)

Place	Date	Hour	Summary of Events and Information	Remarks and references to Appendices
Brentwood	4/10/15		Brigade office notified that Camp would be struck between 18th & 28th inst. move made to Brentwood.	
	5/10/15		3571 Pte McGuiness struck off strength as a deserter.	
	6.		2/Lt. Cale returned to 13th Worc. Regt.	
	"		Pte A. Seale died in hospital of enteric fever.	
	9.		Sir John Brownley having proceeded on leave Col. A.G. Payton assumes command of the Brigade.	
	"		2/Lt. Challe-Frieman reports for duty.	
			Pte. W. Bryson, 2/V. Durkin. (Reading) 2/Lt. Thompson from Artists Rifles. Gazetted 2/Lieutenants.	
			Battalion moves by route march to HATFIELD PEVEREL for Divisional Training, & bivouached there on the 12th.	
	11.		The Battalion remained in Reserve till 4:30, when the Brigade returned to CHELMSFORD.	
	13.		11 men sent to 8.3rd Prov. Battn. on medical ground.	
			Air craft passed over camp at Epping 9.30 p.m. & visited LONDON.	
	14.		Battalion returns to EPPING.	
			Pte. F.A.N. Brown from Artists Rifles (sic) 2/Lt.	
	15.		2/Lt. Melville Smith rebates for duty.	
	18.		2/Lts. Brittan, Durkin, Reading & Thompson (?) joined duty	

Army Form C. 2118.

WAR DIARY
or
INTELLIGENCE SUMMARY.   3/1". WORC. REGT.

(Erase heading not required.)

Instructions regarding War Diaries and Intelligence Summaries are contained in F. S. Regs., Part II. and the Staff Manual respectively. Title pages will be prepared in manuscript.

Place	Date	Hour	Summary of Events and Information	Remarks and references to Appendices
BRENTWOOD	16/9/15		1 Officer transferred to admin. Centre for munition work.	
	22.		2/Lt. Brown reported for duty.	
	23		1 man transferred to admin. Centre for munition work.	
	24		1 man taken on strength from 3/7th Batt?	
	25		Batt? struck camp & marched to BRENTWOOD. 2 watercarts received.	
	26.		Officer Guinness apprehended as a deserter. 1 man transferred to admin. Centre for munition work.	
	29.		1 man discharged medically unfit. Recruit Hancock - 3 men returned from recruiting duty.	

C.W. Thomas
Major 3/1 Worc Regt.

CONFIDENTIAL 2/7" WORC REG Army Form C. 2118.

WAR DIARY
or
INTELLIGENCE SUMMARY.
(Erase heading not required.)

Instructions regarding War Diaries and Intelligence Summaries are contained in F. S. Regs., Part II. and the Staff Manual respectively. Title pages will be prepared in manuscript.

Place	Date	Hour	Summary of Events and Information	Remarks and references to Appendices
BRENTWOOD	Nov 3		Recruit Binder reports in but Divisional Training Scheme	
	5			
	6		6 men sent to 62nd Prov Batt. for Home Service	
	7		1 man discharge M.U. 7th Rl. Smith, transferred to R.E.	
	8		2 men transferred A.C. to munitions	
			5 men transferred from 62nd Prov. B?	
	15		20 NCO's Men sent to WORCESTER for recruiting	
	16		1 man transferred A.C. to munitions	
			3 men " " " " Pass BICESTER recruiting	
	17		1 man to A.C. to munitions. 1 NCO to R Flying Corps	
	21		4 men to 62nd Prov. B? M.S.	
	23		2 men refines from A.C.	
	26		2 men to A.C. to munitions	
	27		2 men to A.C. to munitions. 1 NCO 7 men to 62nd Prov Bn	
			15 Runs men to A.C. - Home Service	
	28		2 men to A.C. to munitions	
	29		1 man to A.C. to munitions	

C.W. Thomas
Lt Col.

CONFIDENTIAL

WAR DIARY OF

2/7th. BATTALION WORCESTERSHIRE REGIMENT

From 1st.DECEMBER 1915 To 31st.DECEMBER 1915

Army Form C. 2118.

WAR DIARY
or
INTELLIGENCE SUMMARY.
(Erase heading not required.)

2/7 Worc Regt

Instructions regarding War Diaries and Intelligence Summaries are contained in F.S. Regs., Part II. and the Staff Manual respectively. Title pages will be prepared in manuscript.

Place	Date	Hour	Summary of Events and Information	Remarks and references to Appendices
BRENTWOOD	1.12.15		2nd Lts. HILL, FLINT, BRITTON, READING transferred to 3rd Line	2/15
"	2.12.15		Company training.	2/15
"	3.12.15		Company training.	2/15
"	4.12.15	9.0 A.M.	Battalion route march. PILGRIM'S HATCH, COXTIE GREEN, SOUTH WEALD COMMON, WEALD CHURCH, BRENTWOOD	2/15
"	5.12.15		Divine service. 1 n.c.o. discharged medically unfit	2/15
"	6.12.15		Company training. Repayment Grenade & trench fighting course commenced under Lt. G.A. THOMPSON	2/15
"	7.12.15		Company training.	2/15
"	8.12.15	9.0 A.M.	Battalion went to day trenches at MOUNT-NESSING.	2/15
"	9.12.15		Company training. 1 n.c.o. transferred to A.C. (munitions).	2/15
"	10.12.15		Company training. 1 n.c.o. transferred to A.C. (munitions). 14 Boysmen transferred to 3rd Line	2/15
"	11.12.15	9.0 A.M.	Battalion route march. GALLOWS GREEN, CANTERBURY TYE, BANNISTER'S FARM, SWALLOWS CROSS, MOUNT-NESSING, SHENFIELD, BRENTWOOD 10 miles.	2/15
"	12.12.15		Divine service.	2/15
"	13.12.15		Company training.	2/15
"	14.12.15		Company training. MAJOR E.W. THOMAS transferred to 3rd line. CAPT. E.H. GRAINGER taken over the duties of 2nd in Command and 1 n.c.o. to 3rd Line. 1 n.c.o. transferred to A.C. (munitions). 11 men transferred to B 2nd Line. Pvt. Bolton	2/15
"	15.12.15		Company training. 2nd Lt. BOOKER appointed assistant M.G.O.	2/15
"	16.12.15		Company training.	2/15
"	17.12.15		Company training.	2/15
"	18.12.15	9.0 A.M.	BRIGADE route march. EAST HORNDON - MONKS - GREAT WARLEY - STREET - BRENTWOOD. 12 miles.	2/15
"	19.12.15		Divine service. 1 n.c.o. transferred to A.C. (munitions).	2/15
"	20.12.15		Company training.	2/15
"	21.12.15			

Army Form C. 2118.

WAR DIARY
or
INTELLIGENCE SUMMARY.

(Erase heading not required.) 2/7 Worc. Regt.

Instructions regarding War Diaries and Intelligence Summaries are contained in F. S. Regs., Part II. and the Staff Manual respectively. Title pages will be prepared in manuscript.

Place	Date	Hour	Summary of Events and Information	Remarks and references to Appendices
BRENTWOOD	22.12.15		Company training.	T/S.
"	23.12.15		Company training. 1 NCO discharged to enlisted a commission	T/S.
"	24.12.15		Fatigues	T/S.
"	26.12.15		Divine service. Xmas dinner to NCO's & men & concert at night.	T/S.
"	26.12.15		Divine service	T/S.
"	27.12.15		C.O. watched the parades.	T/S.
"	28.12.15		Company training. 2 men transferred to A.C. (munitions). 2 men transferred to 82nd Prov. Batt. M.U.	T/S.
"	29.12.15		Company training. BOARD of SURVEY on equipment assembled. CAPT. E.H. GRAINGER pursuant. CAPT	T/S.
"			GREEN 2nd Lt BINDER	
"	30.12.15		Company training. SIR J. BARNSLEY goes on leave. COL. PEYTON takes over COMMAND of BRIGADE	T/S.
"	31.12.15		Company training.	T/S.

L. Pheinique. Cpl.
for. O.C. 2/7 Worc Regt

1577 Wt.W10791/1773 500,000 1/15 D. D. & L. A.D.S.S./Forms/C. 2118.

CONFIDENTIAL.

WAR DIARY of

2/7th Battalion THE WORCESTERSHIRE REGIMENT.

FROM 1st JANUARY, 1916, TO 31st JANUARY, 1916.

Army Form C. 2118

WAR DIARY
or
INTELLIGENCE SUMMARY
(Erase heading not required.)

2/7 Mac Regt.

Instructions regarding War Diaries and Intelligence Summaries are contained in F.S. Regs., Part II. and the Staff Manual respectively. Title Pages will be prepared in manuscript.

Place	Date 1916	Hour	Summary of Events and Information	Remarks and references to Appendices
BRENTWOOD	June 1	9.0 a.m.	Shed No. 1. Battalion route march. BRENTWOOD - INGRAVE GREEN - WARLEY - COXTIE GREEN PILGRIM'S HATCH - BRENTWOOD.	BHS. THH
"	" 2		Divine Service - 1 nm transferred to A.C. munitions -	THH
"	" 3		Company training. Col Sir JOHN BARNSLEY returns from tour of munitions & munitions works of Bryans	THH.
"	" 4		Company training. COL PEYTON goes out to FRANCE. CAPT. GRAINGER takes over Command	THH. THS
"	" 5		Company training.	THS
"	" 6		Company training. Instruction in use of entrenching tool.	THS
"	" 7		Company training. 2 men transferred A.C. munitions. 2 men transferred to machinists	THS
"	" 8	9.0	Battalion route march. PILGRIM'S HATCH - MILLFIELD - KELVEDON HATCH - NOOK END - NEW FARM - PETTITS FARM - CANTERBURY TYE. - BRENTWOOD.	THS. THH
"	" 9		Divine Service.	
"	" 10		Company training. Night operations. 6.30 P.M. - 8-30 P.M. Elementary training. Scouting & running	THS. THH
"	" 11		Company training. 1 NCO & 1 man transferred to A.C. munitions	THS.
"	" 12		Company training. Night operations. Entrenching work. 6.30 PM - 8.30 PM.	THS.
"	" 13		Company training. 2 Companies instructed in use of Bno bombs. Lecture by CAPT. GRAINGER & Officers on DEFENCE. 6.30 - 6.15 P.M.	THS.
"	" 14	9.0.	BRIGADE TACTICAL SCHEME. Details attached. Appendix A.	THS
"	" 15		Company training. 1 Company instructed in use of Bno bombs.	THS

Army Form C. 2118

WAR DIARY
or
INTELLIGENCE SUMMARY
(Erase heading not required.)

2/7 War Regt.

Summary of Events and Information

Place	Date	Hour	Summary of Events and Information	Remarks and references to Appendices
BRENTWOOD	1916 Jan 16		Divine Service.	n/s
"	" 17		Company training. 1 Company instructed in use of Bro Helmets. 5 men transferred to A.C. munitions. Lt EDMUND BAYONET FIGHTING Command - Trans from LONDON Brigade 17.1.16.	n/s
			To be Temp Majors EDWARD H GRAINGER dated 19.9.15 GEORGE H GREEN dated 14.12.15	n/s
			To be Temp Majors K.S. HEMMINGWAY – S.C. BOOKER – S.H. PREET. dated 15.9.15	n/s
			2nd Lts to be Temp Lts L.W. HANCOX. dated 14.12.15	n/s
			To be Hon. Captain.	n/s
"	" 18		Company training.	n/s
"	" 19		Company training. 1 man transferred to A.C. munitions. District Inspecting Supervisor ap.	n/s
			GYMNASTICS inspected Battalion.	
"	" 20		MAJOR GENERAL DIXON inspected the Battalion. 1 man transferred to A.C. munitions	n/s
"	" 21		DRAFT of 324 men joined from 3rd line.	n/s
			Company training. Recruits musketry instruction	
"	" 22		Regimental exercise. Short hostile exercise for officers.	n/s
"	" 23		Divine Service. 2 men transferred to A.C. munitions	n/s
"	" 24		Company training.	n/s
"	" 25		Company training. G.O.C. inspected recruits. 1 Gymnastic Instructor attached to the Battalion from ALDERSHOT.	n/s
"	" 26		Company training – Medical Board as not officers	n/s
"	" 27		BRIGADE FIELD DAY. Show attached. (1 man transferred to A.C. munitions. Appendix B	n/s

WAR DIARY
or
INTELLIGENCE SUMMARY.

(Erase heading not required.)

2/7 Manc Regt

Army Form C. 2118

Place	Date 1916	Hour	Summary of Events and Information	Remarks and references to Appendices
BRENTWOOD	Jan 28		Sheet No. 3. Company training. 1 mm transferred to A.C. munitions. 1 mm discharged unfit.	2/Lt.
	" 29		Battalion route march & wheeled vehicles SHENFIELD - INGRAVE - WARLEY - GT. BROOKE	2/Lt.
	" 30		Sr. Battalion exercises in rapid deployment under machine gun fire. Divine Service. 1 mm discharged unfit.	2/Lt / 2/Lt.
	" 31		Company training. 150 mm transf. expiry.	

J. Heminque. Major.
for O.C. 2/7 Manc Regt.

Army Form C. 2118.

WAR DIARY
or
INTELLIGENCE SUMMARY

2/7 Manc Regt.

(Erase heading not required.)

Place	Date	Hour	Summary of Events and Information	Remarks and references to Appendices
BRENTWOOD.			Sheet No. 4.	
			Tactical Scheme 12.1.16.	
			BRIGADE ORDERS & BATTALION ORDERS attached.	Appendix A.
			The Battalion with the LEFT Section of 2 defensive guns in with L1 machine guns.	
			Division were made after the operation. The Battalion got home at 4-45 P.M.	
			No comments have been received on the work done.	
			Atthumaga. Mipa.	
			for V.C 2/7 Mnc Regt	
			31.1.16	

Appendix "A" B.

TACTICAL EXERCISE 27th JANUARY, 1916.

2/7th Battalion WORCESTERSHIRE REGIMENT.

Operation Orders by

Colonel A. G. Peyton.

OPERATION ORDERS
BY COLONEL A.G.PEYTON
COMMANDING 2/7th WORCESTER REGT.

Copy No. 2.

BRENTWOOD.
26.1.16.

No. 3.

Ref. 1" O.S. Sheet 108.

---

1. An invading force of all arms reached EAST HORNDON on the night Jan. 26/27, and has taken up an entrenched position in the South end of HORNDON PARK.

2/1st R.F.A.Bde.
183rd Inf. Bde.
2/3rd (S.M) F.Amb.

2. A Force composed as per margin under the Command of Col. Sir J. Barnsley, V.D., is ordered to attack the enemy, and either destroy or capture him.

3. The Place of assembly will be at SHENFIELD 10 a.m. at the junction of the SHENFIELD - BILLERICAY road with the main CHELMSFORD - LONDON road by second N in INN.

4. The route will be SHENFIELD - PRIEST LANE (the road cutting the D in BRENTWOOD) - SHENFIELD COMMON - INGRAVE GREEN.

5. The starting point will be on the LONDON - CHELMSFORD road at the cross roads West of B in BRENTWOOD.

6. The head of the main body will pass the starting point at 9.45 a.m. order as per margin.

2 Co.s 2/6 Glos.R.
 (Advance Guard)
Hdqrs.183rd Inf.Bde.
2/6th Glosters (less 2 Co.s)
2/7th Worcesters
2/8th Worcesters
2/4th Glosters
183rd Inf. Bde. S.A.A. reserve
 (under Major Gwynne)
2/3rd (S.M) Field Ambulance.

7. 2 Cyclists will report to O.C. Advance Guard at the starting point 9.30 a.m.

Scouts
Signallers
Pioneers
 D.
 A.
 B.
 C.
Machine Guns.
1st line Transport.

8. The Battalion as per margin will parade in column of route in the ONGAR road at 9.45 a.m. The head of the column will be on the junction of the ONGAR road with the LONDON - CHELMSFORD road.

9. The Transport Officer will arrange for 2 S.A.A. carts to join the S.A.A. reserve.
10. Drummers will parade with their Companies.
11. The 16 stretcher bearers with the stretchers will be with their Companies.
12. Cookers and Water carts will not be taken.
13. Ammunition supply will be practised in the Field, and the attention of all Officers, Regtl. Sgt. Major, and Company Sgt. Majors and Quartermaster Sgts. is directed to I.T. section 165 and 166.

(Signed) F. Dudley Simpson, Capt.& Adjt.
2/7th Battn. Worcestershire Regt.

Copy No.1 to O.C.2/7th Worc.R.
 "   " 2 to Major Grainger
 "   " 3 to Adjutant
 "   " 4 to O.C. 'A' Coy.
 "   " 5 to O.C. 'B' Coy.
 "   " 6 to O.C. 'C' Coy.
 "   " 7 to O.C. 'D' Coy.
 "   " 8 to O.C. Signallers
 "   " 9 to O.C. Transport
 "   " 10 to Quartermaster
 "   " 11 to Machine Gun Officer
 "   " 12 to Regtl. S.M.
 "   " 13   File

Army Form C. 2118.

WAR DIARY
or
INTELLIGENCE SUMMARY
(Erase heading not required.)

2/7 Worc Regt.   Appendix B

Place	Date	Hour	Summary of Events and Information	Remarks and references to Appendices
BRENTWOOD			Show No. 5	2/7
			Operation orders issued by Col. A.G. PEYTON 26.1.16.	
			The Battalion took the left section of attack. Weather was bad and foggy + the work extremely difficult. Blank was used for the 1st time. The recruits proceeded well the Battalion & consequently the work was enjoyed. The Battalion got right round the right flank of the enemy towards the close of operations. No comments have been received so far on the work done.	

T. Thrupp. Major
for O.C. 2/7 Worc Regt.

Appendix "A"

TACTICAL EXERCISE 14th JANUARY, 1916.

183rd BRIGADE.

Operation Orders by

Brigadier General Sir John Barnsley V.D.

SUBJECT – Tactical Exercise
on Jan 14/16.

FROM
    Headquarters,
       183rd. Infantry Brigade.

TO
    Officer Commanding –

       2/1st. R.F.A. Brigade.
       2/4th. Gloucester R.
       2/6th. Gloucester R.
       2/7th. Worcester R.
       2/8th. Worcester R.
       2/3rd. (South Mid:) Field Ambulance.

BRENTWOOD.   10.1.16.

       The Brigade will take part in a Tactical Exercise on Friday next the 14th. inst.,

Reference ½" O.S. Sheet 30.

General Idea.   On the night 13/14 January, 1916 the 61st. Division is billeted in the neighbourhood of BRENTWOOD. An invading force of all arms has landed at SOUTHEND and is moving on BILLERICAY with the apparent intention of cutting the LONDON main line of railway.

Special Idea.   A column composed of –

       2/1st. R.F.A. Brigade,
       183rd. Infantry Brigade,
       2/3rd. (South Mid:) Field Ambulance,

under the command of Col. SIR JOHN BARNSLEY V.D. is ordered to be at BILLERICAY at 11 a.m. on the morning of January 14th. 1916, to take up a defensive position to the S.E. of that town, and to delay the enemy until the Division has taken up a defensive position along the main line of railway. *Enemy scouts will be at RAYLEIGH at 8.0 a.m. on Jan 14th 1916.*

       (Sgd) M.Marriott, Major.
   Brigade Major, 183rd. Infantry Brigade.

OPERATION ORDER NO. 37.

BY COL. SIR JOHN BARNSLEY V.D.

COMMANDING 183rd. Infantry Brigade.

Copy No. 5.

Brentwood.

11.1.16.

Reference ½" O.S. Sheet 30

1. On the night 13/14 January, 1916 the 61st. Division is billeted in the neighbourhood of BRENTWOOD. An invading force of all arms has landed at SOUTHEND and is moving on BILLERICAY with the apparent intention of cutting the LONDON main line of Railway.

2/1st. R.F.A. Bde.
183rd. Infantry Bde.
2/3rd. (South Midland) Field Ambulance.

2. A column composed as per margin under the command of COL. SIR JOHN BARNSLEY V.D. will be at BILLERICAY at 11 a.m. on the morning of January 14th. 1916, and take up a defensive position to the S.E. of that town, delaying the enemy until the Division has taken up a defensive position along the main line of Railway.

3. The column will rendezvous at the road Junction on the SHENFIELD - BILLERICAY road, at 10.45 a.m East of point 166.

2/1st. R.F.A. Bde.

4. The 2/1st. R.F.A. Brigade will proceed via LAWNESS. The remainder via SHENFIELD and HUTTON.

183rd. Infantry Bde.
2/3rd. (South Midland) Field Ambulance.

5. The starting point for the 183rd. Infantry Brigade and the 2/3rd. (South Midland) Field Ambulance will be on the BRENTWOOD - INGATESTONE road, at the Junction of the INGRAVE road.

2 Companies 2/4th. Gloucester R.

6. The Advanced Guard composed as per margin will be ¼ mile ahead of main body.

Headquarters
183rd. Infantry Bde.,
2/4th. Gloucester R.,
(less 2 Companies.),
2/6th. Gloucester R.,
2/7th. Worcester R.,
2/8th. Worcester R.,
183rd. Infantry Bde S.A.A. Reserve,
Brigaded Cookers and Water Carts,
2/3rd. (South Midland) Field Ambulance.

7. The head of the column, order as per margin, will pass the starting point at 9 a.m.

8. The Brigade S.A.A. Reserve will be under the command of Major C.C.Gwynn, 2/4th. Gloucester R.

9. The Cookers and Water Carts will be brigaded under an Officer to be detailed by the Brigade Transport Officer.

10. Each Battalion will detail 2 cyclists to report to O.C. Advanced Guard at starting point at 8.40 a.m.

OPERATION ORDER NO. 37 (Contd)

---

11. All messages to be sent to Headquarters, at the head of column.

(Sgd) M.Marriott, Major.
Brigade Major, 183rd. Infantry Brigade.

Copy No. 1 to Divisional Headquarters - by post.
" " 2 to 2/1st. R.F.A. Brigade - by Orderly.
" " 3 to 2/4th. Gloucester R. - by Orderly.
" " 4 to 2/6th. Gloucester R. - by Orderly.
" " 5 to 2/7th. Worcester R. - by Orderly.
" " 6 to 2/8th. Worcester R. - by Orderly.
" " 7 to 2/3rd. (South Midland) - by Orderly.
      Field Ambulance.

OPERATION ORDERS
BY CAPTAIN E.H.GRAINGER
COMMANDING 2/7th WORCESTER REGT.

Copy No. 2.

BRENTWOOD.
12. 1. 16.

No. 2.

Ref. ½" O.S. Sheet 30.

- -

1. On the night of 13/14 January 1916 the 61st Division is Billeted in the neighbourhood of BRENTWOOD. An invading force of all arms has landed at SOUTHEND and is moving on BILLERICAY with the apparent intention of cutting the LONDON main line of railway.

2. A column composed as per margin under the Command of Colonel Sir John Barnsley, V.D. will be at BILLERICAY at 11 a.m. on the morning of January 14th 1916, and take up a defensive position to the S.E. of that town, delaying the enemy until the Division has taken up a defensive position along the main line of railway.

2/1st.R.F.A.Bde.
183rd Inf. Bde.
2/3rd (S.M) Fld.
   Ambulance.

3. The Column will rendezvous at the road junction on the SHENFIELD - BILLERICAY road at 10.45 a.m. E. of point 166.

4. The starting point of the 183rd Infantry Brigade will be the BRENTWOOD - INGATESTONE road at the junction of the INGRAVE road.

2 Companies
2/4th Glosters.

5. The advance guard as per margin will be ¾ a mile ahead of the main body.

6. The head of the column, order as per margin, will pass the starting point at 9 a.m.

Hdqrs.183rd
  Inf. Bde.
2/4th Glosters.
 less 2 Co.'s
2/6th Glosters.
2/7th Worcesters.
2/8th Worcesters.
183rd.Inf.Bde.S.A.A.Reserve.
Brigaded Cookers & Water Carts.
2/3rd (S.M) Field Ambulance.

7. The Battalion as per margin will parade in the ONGAR ROAD facing S.E. at 9 a.m. on 14th January 1916, the head of the column on the main BRENTWOOD - INGATESTONE Road. Pack mules will parade with their Companies. Drummers will parade with their Companies.

Scouts.
Signallers.
Pioneers.
  A.
  B.
  C.
  D.
Machine Guns.
1st line Transport, less 2 S.A.A.Carts, Water
  carts & cookers.

8. O.C.Signallers will detail 2 cyclist orderlies to report to O.C.Advance Guard at starting point at 8.40 a.m.

9. The Brigade S.A.A. reserve will be under the Command of Major G.C.Gwynne, 2/4th Glosters. The Transport Officer will detach 2 S.A.A. carts from the 1st line transport to form the Brigade S.A.A. Reserve.

10. The Cookers and Water Carts will be brigaded under an Officer to be detailed by the Brigade Transport Officer. Dinners will be cooked on the way and be ready for issue at 12 noon.

11. The Transport will be fully loaded with the exception of the ammunition. Ammunition will not be taken.

```
Copy No.1 To O.C.2/7th Worc.R.    Copy No.7 to O.C.Signallers
  "   "  2 "  Adjutant              "    "  8  " O.C.Transport.
  "   "  3 "  O.C. 'A' Coy.         "    "  9  " Quartermaster.
  "   "  4 "  O.C. 'B' Coy.         "    " 10  " Machine Gun Officer.
  "   "  5 "  O.C. 'C' Coy.         "    " 11  " Regtl. S. M.
  "   "  6 "  O.C. 'D' Coy.         "    " 12    File.
```

CONFIDENTIAL

War diary of.

2/7th 13th the Worcestershire Regiment.

from 23rd May 1916 to 31st May 1916.

Volume 1

WAR DIARY or INTELLIGENCE SUMMARY

(Erase heading not required.)   2/4 Bn The Wiltshire Regt.

Army Form C. 2118

Place	Date	Hour	Summary of Events and Information	Remarks and references to Appendices
TIDWORTH	23.5.16		The Bn moved to SOUTHAMPTON. 2 Trains (1) X1447. 19 Officers 441 O.R. (2) X1449. 18 Officers 485 O.R.	1 F. 4 F.
SOUTHAMPTON		6 p.m.	Embarked on CAESAREA. for HAVRE	4 F.
SOUTHAMPTON	24.5.16	9 a.m.	Returned to dock having been warned of Submarine when just outside HAVRE	4 F.
HAVRE	25.5.16	3.45 a.m.	Arrived at HAVRE. 5 men left in Hospital at HAVRE	7 F.
		7.30 a.m.	Disembarked.	7 F.
		11.10 a.m.	Rest Camp No 1.	2 men left in Hospital 7 F.
HAVRE	26.5.16		Left HAVRE in 2 Trains to BERGUETTE (1) 13 Officers b 7 men 250 men (2) 6 Officers 250 men at HAVRE	4 F.
ROBECQ	27.5.16		Detrained at BERGUETTE + marched to ROBECQ	7 F.
	28.5.16	12 noon	Church Parade. Address by XI Army Corps Commander at ST VENANT	4 F.
	29.5.16		Inspection by 1st Army Commander. Company route marches	4 F.
	30.5.16		Billets at ROBECQ	7 F.
VIEILLE CHAPPELLE	31.5.16		Marched from ROBECQ to VIEILLE CHAPPELLE in Billets at VIEILLE CHAPPELLE	7 F.

S.T.Ohman Lt Col.
Comdg. 2/4 Bn. Wiltshire Regt.

Army Form C. 2118

WAR DIARY
or
INTELLIGENCE SUMMARY 2/4th 1/3rd The Worcestershire Regt.

(Erase heading not required.)

Instructions regarding War Diaries and Intelligence Summaries are contained in F.S. Regs., Part II. and the Staff Manual respectively. Title Pages will be prepared in manuscript.

Place	Date	Hour	Summary of Events and Information	Remarks and references to Appendices
VIEILLE CHAPELLE	1.6.16		A, B & C-D Companies attached to 105 Inf Brigade in FERME DU BOIS section to instruction. B Coy to 1st LANCS. FUSILIERS. C Coy to 18th LANCS FUSILIERS. D Coy to 20th LANCS FUSILIERS Right Sector LEFT Sector. left Coy in Reserve RICHEBOURG ST VAAST	1D
VIEILLE CHAPELLE	2.6.16.		Headquarters + A Coy attached to 23rd MANCHESTERS for instruction (Right Company in reserve) LA TOURET.	7D
"	3.6.16.		1NCO + 3 men attended sniping course at STEENBECQUE. 3 NCO's attended Anti gas school at AIRE	7D
"	4.6.16		Trench routine	7D
"	5.6.16		B. Company relieved by C. Company in LEFT Sector FERME DU BOIS.	7D
"	6.6.16		C Company reprs. 1 casualty (killed). A Company relieve D Company in RIGHT Sector FERME DU BOIS.	7D
"	7.6.16		C Company in Left Sector. A Company in Right Sector FERME DU BOIS. A Company in support at LE TOURET. B " " " " " at RICHEBOURG	?
"	8.6.16	2pm	B + D Companies relieved by 2 Companies 2/6 GLOSTER REGT & returned to VIEILLE CHAPELLE	?
"	9.6.16		A + C Companies relieved by "	?
"	10.6.16.		Battalion concentrated at VIEILLE CHAPELLE.	?
PONT DU HEM	11.6.16		Marched via ETON ROAD to PONT DU HEM. Took over Billets from 14th ROYAL WELCH FUSILIERS. in support to left sector of MOATED GRANGE Section.	?
	12.6.16		Billets at PONT DU HEM	?
	13.6.16			?
	14.6.16			?
	15.6.16			?

WAR DIARY
or
INTELLIGENCE SUMMARY

(Erase heading not required.)

2/7/15 The WORCESTERSHIRE REGT.

Army Form C. 2118

Place	Date	Hour	Summary of Events and Information	Remarks and references to Appendices
NEUVE-CHAPELLE	16.6.16		Daylight relief of 15"(S) Bn CHESHIRE REGT in NEUVE-CHAPELLE Section. NO casualties. Line taken over from S.5.2.16 M 35.3.	
	17.6.16		In trenches - NEUVE CHAPELLE Section. 3 companies in front line, 1 company in reserve in B. LINES	
	18.6.16		In trenches. Trench routine.	
	19.6.16		" " Trench routine. No casualty, slightly retrenched.	
	20.6.16		Artillery bombardment of enemy front line trenches. Patrols established by Hun. or Enemy steam MERVILLE. 3 casualties. 2 dit Jeremade	
	21.6.16		Daylight relief by 2/8" WARWICK'S relief completed by 3.55pm no casualties marched to LA GORGUE into Divisional rest.	
LA GORGUE	22.6.16		Rest. Cleaning kit.	
	23.6.16		Rest. Company's made complete Comm trench. Bombers. Bayonet fighting musketry class. Osb. class	
	24.6.16		"	
	25.6.16		"	
	26.6.16		"	
	27.6.14		"	
	28.6.16		"	
	29.6.16		"	
	30.6.16		"	

CONFIDENTIAL.

War Diary

- of -

2/7th Bn Worcestershire Regt.

From 1st July 1916 to 31st July 1916

Vol. 3.

No. 1.

Army Form C. 2118.

Instructions regarding War Diaries and Intelligence Summaries are contained in F.S. Regs., Part II. and the Staff Manual respectively. Title pages will be prepared in manuscript.

WAR DIARY
or
INTELLIGENCE SUMMARY.
(Erase heading not required.)

2/7 Worcestershire Regt.

Place	Date	Hour	Summary of Events and Information	Remarks and references to Appendices
LAGORGUE	July 1		Rest Billets. Companies under Coy Commanders. O.R. W.1 wounded (rifle)	S.H.G.
	" 2		Capt + Adjt. F.D. SIMPSON goes into hospital (piles). Lieut. A.H. BOWMAN is appointed Bombing Officer vice Lieut. THOMPSON. O.R. K.1 wounded 2 (all with 61st Div. MINING T.A. Lieut. J. MANUEL takes over duties as M.O.	
TAUQUISSART RIGHT SECTOR	" 3		Relieved 2/5th LOS. REGT. TOOK over TAUQUISSART R. Sect of LINE. work in trenches. 10 to 10.30 P.M. Heavy bombardment of ENEMY LINE 10.30 P.M. 1 Company +	S.H.G. S.H.G.
	" 4		2 M.Gs entered GERMAN trenches at NIGHT. 6. did considerable damage with bombs to GERMANS in trenches + flying M.Gs. Thr party left the GERMAN LINES at 11.20 P.M. + were all back at 11.30 P.M. artillery, caused bombardment till 12.0 P.M. 4 officers wounded. Capt. HOPEWELL E.R. Capt. TOMKINSON G.S. 2nd LIEUT BINDER A.E.L. 9 2nd LIEUT THOMPSON J.G. O.R.K.2 W.3 1 Trench warfare. Heavy bombardment 10.0 P.M. to 10.30 P.M. considerable damage to ENEMY'S parapet + wire. Capt HANCOCKS W takes over command of D Coy vice Capt. HOPEWELL wounded. O.R.W.4 (accidentally)	S.H.G.
	" 5		Quiet day. usual bombardment 10.0 P.M. to 10.30 P.M. O.R.W.4.	S.H.G. S.H.G.
	" 6		Considerable artillery fire from ENEMY during day to which we replied. Usual bombardment 10.0 P.M. to 10.30 P.M. Also at intervals during the night - at 1.45 P.M. on wire. O.R.W.1.	
	" 7		2nd LIEUT DURKIN F.V. joins to B/d R.E. 5½ pillars.	S.H.G.
	" 8		Trench routine. usual artilling on both sides. O.R.W. 6.	S.H.G.
	" 9		The following officers posted to battalion report for duty. 2nd LIEUT.s G.M.I. BLACKBURNE, H.J. PADDISON, R.W. SELLERS, J.A. LAWRENCE, R.B. BERRY, T.A.L. WARRINER & J.H. ROBINSON. O.R.K. W.1.	S.H.G.
	" 10		Morning relief by 2/6 WORCESTERS commenced 5 a.m. completed 3.0 P.M. proceed into BIV.	S.H.G.
LAVENTIE	" 11		REST BILLETS at LAVENTIE. O.R.W.1. 2 men rejoined.	S.H.G.
	" 12		Bathing + inspections. 3 men rejoined. Working parties. 4 men evacuated sick to ENGLAND	S.H.G.

1577 Wt.W10791/1773 500,000 1/15 D.D.&L. A.D.S.S./Forms/C. 2118.

No 2

Army Form C. 2118

Instructions regarding War Diaries and Intelligence Summaries are contained in F.S. Regs., Part II. and the Staff Manual respectively. Title Pages will be prepared in manuscript.

783 ed

2/7 Worc Regt

WAR DIARY or INTELLIGENCE SUMMARY

(Erase heading not required.)

Place	Date July	Hour	Summary of Events and Information	Remarks and references to Appendices
LAVENTIE	13		Working parties. 2 reported from hospital.	7/146
	14		" " Special training for 60 men (for raid)	
	15		Hospital. MAJOR GRAIN GER takes men command of the battalion O.R.W. 2 (wrk 183 - 2TM 3). 2nd L+ Col DORMAN L.C. goes into	7/146
			Working parties. MAJOR GREEN became 2nd in command. LIEUT GROVE taken over command of B Coy vice MAJOR GREEN. LIEUT BEROBERTS is appointed company officer vice LIEUT GROVE O.R.W. 10. 2nd LIEUT BRODIE is appointed Bde Salvage Officer O.R.W. 10. LIEUT E.C. HEMINGWAY goes into hospital sick. 2 reported from hospital. 1 sent to base (wia orw 4/c)	7/146
	16		Working parties. 2nd LIEUT WARRINER enters hospital sick	7/146
	17		" 2 reported from hospital	7/146
	18		O.R.W. 2.	7/146
FAUQUISSART LEFT SECTOR	19		Battery of artillery to until we commenced relieving 2/4 + 2/6 GLOUCESTERS at ~ 10 p.m. on left sector of FAUQUISSART SECTION N14.A.N 13.7	7/146
	20		Completed relief of 2/4 + 2/6 GLOUCESTERS at 2 a.m. Repaired parapets between NO MAN'S LAND & clearly dead to rebuild in trenches O.R.W. 1. Wounded & died from base abdominal wounded sick to ENGLAND. Brought in wounded 28 men (2/4 GLOS) from NO MAN'S LAND during daylight; also wounded officer (LIEUT METCALFE 2/4 GLOS) + dead men after startled at sniper. Repairing parapets & collected patrols O.R.W. 1	7/146
	21			
	22		Send routine. Batt. H.Q. vacated & moved to H.Q. [crossed]. 2 Batteries between from an immediate front. Re-wiring front and aid O.R.W. in addition to front already occupied today was relieved) The 2/H - Batt. O + B	7/146
	23		L.T. of the 184 Hyd. with C + D Coys on line being thus extended on left to N 8 d 18. Trench routine & re-wiring the front continued. END POST, being relieved by 2/8 S Wors. CAPT BUTCHER killed on return night of 23/7/16 O.R.W. 2	7/146

No. 3.

Army Form C. 2118.

WAR DIARY
or
INTELLIGENCE SUMMARY.

2/7 Worc Regt

(Erase heading not required.)

Place	Date July	Hour	Summary of Events and Information	Remarks and references to Appendices
FAUQUISSART LEFT SECTOR	24		Trench routine. Re-wiring front entained. 2/6 GLOUCESTERS sent party to retrieve Men dead from NO MAN'S LAND & bury them. We supplied wiring party O.R.K.W.7	3.14.6
	25		Trench routine. Re-wiring front entained. 2/6 GLOUCESTERS gave out party to retrieve men dead from NO MAN'S LAND & bury them. We supplied covering party. Thoroughly examined condition of men in front 2nd LIEUT JOHN-STON died of wounds (received on the night of 7th 24/25th) in 1/2nd LONDON C.C.S. MERVILLE. O.R.W.1.	3.14.6
	26		Relief by 2/4 GLOUCESTERS commenced at 5 p.m. & completed by 9.30 p.m. DEADEND, HOUGOUMONT & PICANTIN POSTS taken over from 2/8th WORCESTERS & occupied by 1 Platoon each. Also JOCK'S POST taken over at same Time & occupied by 1 Section	3.14.6
	27		Working parties. Bathing. A Coy relieved by 2/4 Glouc Regt on the 26th. B Coy took over WANGERIE, MASSELOT & ROADBEND POSTS in the afternoon from 2/4 Glouc Regt. LIEUT HAWTREY G.H.C. & 2nd LIEUT HILL E.W. reported for duty. O.R.W. 1 attack(?) 1 63rd 183rd L.T.M.B.	7.14.6
	28		Working parties. Notified from base O.R. H. evacuated sick to ENGLAND 1 Sergt. transferred to A.S.C. 1 man sent to ENGLAND for mining	3.14.6
	29		Working parties. Notified by DIV. Detachment O.R.W. 1 on the 2nd = 1 Cloy absent B Coy	5.14.6
	30		Working parties. " " " " " " in Divn. Posts.	5.14.6
	31		Working parties. D Coy relieves C Coy in above posts WANGERIE, MASSELOT ROAD BEND.	5.14.6

Supplement to

WAR DIARY or INTELLIGENCE SUMMARY

of July, August & Sept? 2/7 Worcestershire Regt

Army Form C. 2118

(Erase heading not required.)

Place	Date	Hour	Summary of Events and Information	Remarks and references to Appendices
Awarded	28.7.16		Honours awarded to Officers & Men not previously included in the War Diaries of July, August & September.	
"	15.8.16		Capt. E.R. Hopewell — Military Cross	
"	15.8.16		10208 Cpl E.T. Beakway — " Medal	
"	23.8.16		10458 L/Cpl G. Tyler — " "	
"	23.8.16		Lieut S.C. Booker — " "	
"	23.8.16		2/Lieut L. Johnston — " "	
"	15.8.16		2/Lieut H.J. Paddison — " "	
"	15.8.16		2687 Sgt A. Preston — Parchment	
"	6.9.16		5718 Pte R. Toms — "	
			1766 Pte A. Hepwood — Military Medal	

L P Norman Lt Col
2/1 Worc R
2/1

Supplement to

WAR DIARIES of July August & Sep?
INTELLIGENCE SUMMARY 2/7 Worcestershire Regt

Army Form C. 2118

(Erase heading not required.)

Place	Date	Hour	Summary of Events and Information	Remarks and references to Appendices
Awards	28/7/16		Honours awarded to Officers & men – previously included in the War Diaries of July August & September	
"	15.8.16		Capt. E.R. Hopewell Military Cross	5/115
"	15.8.16		1:2008 Cpl E.T Blakeway " "	5/115
"	15.8.16		10:1518 L/Cpl C. TYLER " "	5/115
"	23.8.16		Lieut S.C. BOOKER " "	5/115
"	23.8.16		2/Lieut L JOHNSTON " "	5/115
"	23.8.16		2/Lieut H.J. PADDISON " "	5/115
"	15.8.16		2687 Sergt. A PRESTON Parchment	5/115
"	15.8.16		3716 Pte R TOMS "	5/115
"	6.9.16		1766 Pte A.H. ATWOOD Military Medal	2/115

183rd Inf. Bde

War Diary.
- of -
7th Battn. The Worcestershire Regt.

Augt 1st — 31st 1916.

Army Form C. 2118

WAR DIARY
or
INTELLIGENCE SUMMARY

No. 1

247 Worc Regt

(Erase heading not required.)

Instructions regarding War Diaries and Intelligence Summaries are contained in F.S. Regs., Part II. and the Staff Manual respectively. Title Pages will be prepared in manuscript.

Place	Date	Hour	Summary of Events and Information	Remarks and references to Appendices
LAVENTIE	1.8.16		Relieved 2/8 WORC in R sector of FAUQUISSART Salient. 1 Vickers MGunner 2 Batt. 2 Prkto S.H.A 10 Rifles 1 Very Pistol. Bomb Patrol Engagement from NO MANS LAND	T.H.S
FAUQUISSART	2.8.16		Trench relieving. Casualties 1 OR wounded. 150 yds of front wired.	T.H.S
	3.8.16		450 RIFLE GRENADES fired into front works. Between 10 a.m. & 5 a.m. 260 yds of front wired.	T.H.S
	4.8.16		Shelled by enemy 5.9 f. 2 hrs in afternoon. Casualties O.R. Wounded 2. 100 yds of front wired	T.H.S
	5.8.16		Relieved by 2/8 WORC in SUPPORT at LAVENTIE. D.G. in POSTS WINTERIE MAZELOT & ROAD BEND with 1 LEWIS GUN Casualties. Wounded O.R. 2	ed.
LAVENTIE	6.8.16		Working parties. Bathing. A.B. gun turrets at FAUQUISSART B.G in post. 1 NCO killed 2 OR wounded	T.H
	7.8.16		WORKING PARTIES. Bathing. 1 NCO wounded. MAJOR WHITFIELD took over temporary command of Batt.	T.H.
	8.8.16		Working parties. Bathing. C.B. in POSTS	T.H.
LE GRAND PAC -QUOT	9.8.16		Relieved by 5 GLOS Regt. at 4.30 a.m. March to LE GRAND PACQUOT via L. BERGUE arrived 10.15 P.M. 1 O.R. wounded to ENGLAND	T.H
	10.8.16		Companies completed by MAJOR WHITFIELD settling down in billets	T.H

Army Form C. 2118

WAR DIARY
or
INTELLIGENCE SUMMARY   2/7 Worc. Regt.

(Erase heading not required.)

No 2

Instructions regarding War Diaries and Intelligence Summaries are contained in F. S. Regs, Part II. and the Staff Manual respectively. Title Pages will be prepared in manuscript.

Place	Date	Hour	Summary of Events and Information	Remarks and references to Appendices
LE GRAND PACAUT	11.8.16		Company training. Battng. Casualties NIL.	G.H.Q.
	12.8.16		Firing on LE SART Range. Battery keep Groups practice in opening line. Casualties NIL.	G.H.Q.
	13.8.16		Church Parade. Major Green Takes over duties as 2d in command. Capt M. Bynner takes over command of "B" Coy. Casualties Nil	G.H.Q.
	14.8.16		Practising the attack 7 to 9 a.m. The Bynner being present. 11am to 1pm the G.O.C. being present. Casualties Nil.	G.H.Q.
	15.8.16		Batt: Route march. B/de. three hours. The Batt: awarded three prizes. Rifle + shooting 2nd prize. Harnessing + driving 1st 2nd prize. Wrestling on horseback 3rd prize. Casualties NIL.	G.H.Q.
	16.8.16		Aeroplane Signalling. Supervised school. Training as per programme. Battng AC 1-3pm. Casualties NIL	G.H.Q.
	17.8.16		Batt: left LAGRAND PACAUT 2.30 pm marched to CROIX BARBEE. Corps a/ms Cpl Blackwell G Coy awarded military medal. Lt Speak reports. Casualties NIL.	G.H.Q.
NEUVECHAPELLE	18.8.16		Relieved 11th EAST LANCS in NEUVE CHAPELLE sector RT sector Relief completed 12.45 p.m. 2. 2/5th Warwicks men joined from Base. Casualties NIL	G.H.Q.
	19.8.16		Trench routine. Casualties wounded O.R.1	G.H.Q.
	20.8.16		Trench routine. Casualties, wounded OR 2 when wiring.	G.H.Q.
	21.8.16		Trench routine. Casualties wounded OR 2	G.H.Q.
	22.8.16		Relieved by 2/8 Worcs. Relief complete 11.30 a.m. Casualties wounded OR 1 Gassed OR 1	G.H.Q.
CROIX BARBEE			St VAAST ANGLE + GROTTO POSTS with A Coy relieving 2/8 Worcs	
	23.8.16		Training Programme. Battng. Drainage. 2 platoons 4.2 Trenches to 1/7 Batt. Base rejoined us 3 wounded + 4 sick evacuated to ENGLAND. Casualties N12.	G.H.Q.
	24.8.16		Training Programme. 3 shells dropped in St VAAST POST killing one man 6.15 p.m. two other casualties G.H.Q.	
	25.8.16		Lt Col DORMAN Takes over command. Major WHITFIELD goes to Div School. Casualties NIL	G.H.Q.

WAR DIARY
of
INTELLIGENCE SUMMARY 2/7 Worc Regt

No. 3

Army Form C. 2118

Instructions regarding War Diaries and Intelligence Summaries are contained in F.S. Regs., Part II. and the Staff Manual respectively. Title Pages will be prepared in manuscript.

(Erase heading not required.)

Place	Date	Hour	Summary of Events and Information	Remarks and references to Appendices
CROIX BARBÉE	26.8.16		Relieved 2/5" R. Warwicks in Rt Sector MOATED GRANGE section + Posts. 2/4 + Lancaster Regt Battn on left 2/6 = 6 Leicesters Battn on right. Relief complete 11.15 a.m. Casualties O.R. 1. wounded accidentally.	S.H.S.
	27.8.16		Trench routine. Casualties Nil.	S.H.S.
	28.8.16		" O.R. 8, including 1 accidentally.	S.H.S.
	29.8.16		" O.R. 1 killed 3 wounded	S.H.S.
	30.8.16		" O.R. 1 wounded	S.H.S.
	31.8.16		" O.R. 1 killed 2 wounded	S.H.S.

F.C. Forman Lt Col
2/7 Worc. Rgt

183/6

Vol 5

183rd Infantry Brigade

War Diary

of

2/7th Worcester Regiment

for

September 1916

WAR DIARY / INTELLIGENCE SUMMARY

Army Form C. 2118

No. 1

2/7 Worc. Regt.

(Erase heading not required.)

Instructions regarding War Diaries and Intelligence Summaries are contained in F.S. Regs., Part II. and the Staff Manual respectively. Title Pages will be prepared in manuscript.

Place	Date	Hour	Summary of Events and Information	Remarks and references to Appendices
MOATED GRANGE	1.9.16		Relieved by 2/8 Worcesters in MOATED GRANGE Right Sector. Relief complete 12 noon. Casualties Nil.	S.H.S.
RIEZ BAILLEUL	2.9.16		Billetted at RIEZ BAILLEUL. Took over 2/8 Glouc. Billets.	S.H.S.
	3.9.16		Inspection of kit to 2nd Lt. WOOLRIDGE & 2nd Lt. M. DAVIDS from from 2/7 Warw Casualties Nil.	S.H.S.
	4.9.16		Church Parade. Batting. Casualties Nil.	S.H.S.
			Classes & Fatigues. Football match v 2/6 Gloster - drawn 1-1. Won Relay Race with 2/6 Gloster. 2nd Lt K.S. HEMINGWAY takes over command of "B" Coy. Capt. M. BIGWOOD goes to Div. School. 2nd Lt H.S. CONSTANTINE joins from 3/7 Worcs. Casualties Nil.	S.H.S.
	5.9.16		Classes. Casualties Nil.	S.H.S.
	6.9.16		Battalion Sports. Casualties Nil.	S.H.S.
MOATED GRANGE	7.9.16		Relieved 2/8 Worcesters in MOATED GRANGE Right Sector. Relief complete 12 noon. Left of Sector M29.H. 2/6 Gloster. Right of Sector M35.3. 13 St Johns & Lancs. Casualties Nil.	S.H.S.
	8.9.16		Trench Routine. Casualties Nil.	S.H.S.
	9.9.16		Trench Routine. Casualties Nil.	S.H.S.
	10.9.16		" " O.R. 1 wounded.	S.H.S.
	11.9.16		" " Relieved by 2/1 Bucks Regt. Relief complete p.m. Casualties O.R. 1 wounded	S.H.S.
LA GORGUE	12.9.16		Took over 2/5 Glo. Billets at LA GORGUE. Casualties Nil.	S.H.S.
	13.9.16		Fatigues. Batting. Casualties Nil.	S.H.S.
	14.9.16		Holiday. Fatigue party 1 Coy. Major E.H. GRAINGER rejoined from leave. Major F. Lt. GREEN on leave. Casualties Nil.	S.H.S.
	15.9.16		Training for programme. Casualties Nil.	S.H.S.
	16.9.16		Practice "ATTACK" "	S.H.S.
NEUVE CHAPELLE	17.9.16		Left LA GORGUE. Relieved 15th West Yorks by 4.15 p.m. in NEUVE CHAPELLE RIGHT SECTOR Casualties Nil. Trench routine. Lt. A. BOWMAN takes over command of "B" Coy. Casualties O.R. 2 wounded.	S.H.S.

Army Form C. 2118

WAR DIARY
Nº 2
or
INTELLIGENCE SUMMARY 2/7 Worc Regt
(Erase heading not required.)

Instructions regarding War Diaries and Intelligence Summaries are contained in F. S. Regs., Part II. and the Staff Manual respectively. Title Pages will be prepared in manuscript.

Place	Date	Hour	Summary of Events and Information	Remarks and references to Appendices
NEUVE CHAPELLE	18.9.16		Trench routine. Casualties O.R. 1 wounded. Lt GOODWIN.H. returns from course & takes over command of 'B' Coy.	(9.a.)
"	19.9.16		Trench routine. Casualties nil.	
"	20.9.16		Trench routine. Relieved by 2/5 WORCESTERS in Right Subsection NEUVE CHAPELLE Section. Relief Complete by 11.57 AM. Casualties O.R. 1 wounded. Battn went into Divisional Reserve at LA FOSSE	(9.a.)
LA FOSSE	21.9.16		Bathing. Medical Inspection. Fatigue Party. Casualties nil. Capt. BOUCHER. W.F. goes on leave. Lt SPREAT S.H. Enters over command of 'A' Coy.	(9.a.)
"	22.9.16		Training as per programme. 'A' Coy moved to CROIX BARBÉE as a working company for Battn in front line. Casualties nil. Major GRAINGER. E.A. goes on leave.	(9.a.)
"	23.9.16		Training as per programme. Fatigues. Casualties nil.	(9.a.)
"	24.9.16		Church Parade. Casualties nil. MAJOR GREEN rejoined from leave. Col. DORMAN went to conference at Boulogne. MAJOR GREEN took over command of the Battn	(9.a.)
"	25.9.16		Fatigue Party. Holiday. Casualties nil.	(9.a.)
NEUVE CHAPELLE	26.9.16		Relieved 2/5 HORCESTERS in right Subsection NEUVE CHAPELLE Section. Relief complete by 11.30 AM. LEFT Battn 2/8 HOSTERS Right Battn 10th EAST YORKS. H.Q. at PONT LOGY. Casualties O.R. 1 wounded (freestocks). 2/Lt BRIDGE J.T. + 2/Lt CHILDE-FREEMAN E.R. taken to R.F.C.	(9.a.)
"	27.9.16		Trench routine; casualties wounded O.R. 4 (inc. 1 on duty).	(9.a.)
"	28.9.16		Trench routine; casualties wounded O.R. 1.	(9.a.)
"	29.9.16		Trench routine. Casualties nil.	(9.a.)
"	30.9.16		Trench routine. Casualties nil.	(9.a.)

E.H. Green Lieut
Comdg 2/7 Worc Regt

18/9/1

Vol 6

183 Inf Bde.

2/7th Worcestershire Regt

War Diary for October 1916

Army Form C. 2118

WAR DIARY
or
INTELLIGENCE SUMMARY

No. 1. 2/7 WORC REGT

(Erase heading not required.)

Instructions regarding War Diaries and Intelligence Summaries are contained in F.S. Regs., Part II, and the Staff Manual respectively. Title Pages will be prepared in manuscript.

Place	Date	Hour	Summary of Events and Information	Remarks and references to Appendices
NEUVE CHAPELLE	2.10.16		Trench routine. 2nd Lieut GUISE, E.S. GREEN, F.C. AMPHLETT RF and STAINTON E joined. + 10 O.R. from Base — Casualties Nil	G.H.Q.
LA FOSSE	3.10.16		Relieved by 4/R. Warwicks completed 11.30 a.m. Cap BOUCHER rejoined from leave. Billets at LA FOSSE. D Coy in working party at CROIX BARBEE. Casualties wounded O.R. 2	G.H.Q.
"	4.10.16		Inspections &c. Casualties Nil	G.H.Q.
"	5.10.16		Classes, fatigue party. B Coy on special training for raid. Casualties Nil	G.H.Q.
"	6.10.16		" " Capt BIGWOOD rejoins from Div.	G.H.Q.
"	7.10.16		School. Casualties Nil. Parade Service " " Left BIGWOOD taken over from	G.H.Q.
NEUVE CHAPELLE	8.10.16		O.C. B Coy. Cap HANCOCKS W. joined to hospital. Casualties Nil. 2/8 left Batt. Relieved 2/8 Worcesters in Right Sector of NEUVE CHAPELLE Sector. Complete 9.15 p.m. Reliefs hour. R.E. Battn. 16/R.Warwicks. D Coy left at LA FOSSE to remain. 2nd Lieut LAWRENCE joins to Hospital. Casualties Nil	G.H.Q.
	9.10.16		Trench Routine. Casualties Nil.	G.H.Q.
	10.10.16		Trench Routine. Casualties wounded O.R. 1 (slight). Southern Division — 1/6 Glos. took over line to OXFORD STREET from 2/7 Worcs. 2/7 Worcs extended Right & Left and hand to BOND STREET for 16th R. Warwicks. Completed 9 p.m. Raid on by battalion. Threw 30 bombs by 1st Cheshires. At 10 p.m. to 10.59 p.m. on D Coy trenches. Enemy turning at 5 H 3 - 5.1. Enemy to interrupt the party was observed in rest of time turning took about hour to from wire to repair damage. The raid was repulsed - killed - Enemy parties L/c. BOOKER MC 24377. Morris & 96 R wounded 2/Lieut SMITH. J & 6 OR	G.H.Q.
	11.10.16		2/Lt R. WELLERS, LSGIHIE 4 OR. French routine. Casualties Nil (except raid)	G.H.Q.
	12.10.16		Trench Routine. Casualties Nil.	G.H.Q.

WAR DIARY

Army Form C. 2118

Instructions regarding War Diaries and Intelligence Summaries are contained in F.S. Regs., Part II. and the Staff Manual respectively. Title Pages will be prepared in manuscript.

INTELLIGENCE SUMMARY 2/7 WOR. R. REGT

No 2

(Erase heading not required.)

Place	Date	Hour	Summary of Events and Information	Remarks and references to Appendices
NEUVE CHAPELLE & CROIX BARBÉE	13.10.16		Trench routine. Wounded O.R. 1	S/145
	14.10.16	11.30am	Relieved by 2/8 Worcesters. Completed 11.30 a.m. Shoots into billets from 2/8 Worcesters at CROIX BARBÉE. B Coy taken to following posts LANSDOWNE, LORETTO, MARIAGE, ST VAAST'S. Draft of 31 arrived in the evening. Casualties Nil	S/145
	15.10.16		R.C. Inspection. Bath. Church Parade. Draft of 66 arrived in the evening. Casualties Nil	S/145
	16.10.16		General Inspection by Tommy. Draft of 53 arrived. Casualties Wnd. 1 O.R. 2 (Accid.)	S/145
	17.10.16		Coy Training. Casualties Nil	S/145
	18.10.16		Coy + Section Training. Casualties Nil	S/145
	19.10.16		Inspection by B.G.C. Casualties Nil	S/145
NEUVE CHAPELLE	20.10.16		Bn moved to CROIX BARBÉE. Relieved 2/6 Worcesters in R.F. Sector, NEUVE CHAPELLE. Relief complete by 11.30 a.m. Casualties Nil	S/145
	21.10.16		Bn Relieved 2/6 W.R. by 1/7th, 1/6 R.Warwicks. Trench Routine. Casualties Wnd. 1 O.R. 1	S/145
	22.10.16		Trench Routine. B.G.C. inspected new dugouts (one of Trench) Casualties N.2	S/145
	23.10.16		Trench Routine. Casualties N.2	S/145
	24.10.16		Trench Routine N.2 2/8 Army Hamilton + Dudoni transferred to R.F.C. Casualties N.2	S/145
	25.10.16		Relieved by 2/8 W.Yks. Complete 11.40 p.m. Troops were billeted at CROIX BARBÉE. Casualties N.2	S/145
ROUGE BARBÉE	26.10.16		Inspection by Bn Commanders. 9½Gen training. Capt BIGWOOD taken over Command of "D" Coy. Lieut GROVE relinquishes it + returns to "C" Coy. Capt SMELLIE taken over Command of "C" Coy. Lieut H. GOODWIN relinquishes Command of "D" Coy and is 2nd Cd "D" Coy. Casualties N.2	S/145
	27.10.16		Battle by the CROIX BARBÉE 9am. B. This taken over by 1st L.R.B. On march to L'ECLAIR via LOCON, RINGES + CONNEHEM + billets there Casualties 10 wd. 1 O.R. + wounded 1 off. + 1 OR DN.	S/145
L'ECLAIR	28.10.16		Boxing. School. accident Inspections. Brigade held in army reserve. 270.R. arrived from Base Casualties N.2	S/145
	29.10.16		Inspection. Brigade Sr. Reynolds Box inspection Casualties N.2	S/145
	30.10.16		Church Parade Service.	S/145
	31.10.16		Company Training. Casualties N.2	S/145

[signatures]

Vol 7 183/61.

War Diary
- of -
2/7th Battn The Worcestershire Regt
- for -
November 1916.

Army Form C. 2118

WAR DIARY
or
INTELLIGENCE SUMMARY

2/7 Worcestershire Regt.

(Erase heading not required.)

No. 1

Instructions regarding War Diaries and Intelligence Summaries are contained in F. S. Regs., Part II. and the Staff Manual respectively. Title Pages will be prepared in manuscript.

Place	Date	Hour	Summary of Events and Information	Remarks and references to Appendices
L'ECLÊME Cauchy-a-la-Tour	1.11.16		Battn. marched off from L'ECLÊME at 8 a.m. for CAUCHY-A-LA-TOUR (about 8 miles) and billetted there for the night. Casualties Nil.	G.H.Q.
MARQUAY	2.11.16		Battn. marched off at 8 a.m. for MARQUAY arriving 3 p.m. (about 13 miles) Billetted there for the night. Casualties Nil.	G.H.Q.
VILLERS-BRULIN	3.11.16		Battn. marched off 10 a.m. for VILLERS-BRULIN (about 7 miles) Casualties Nil.	G.H.Q.
	4.11.16		Training including Trench Corridors. Casualties Nil.	G.H.Q.
MONT-EN-TERNOIS	5.11.16		Battn. marched off at 11 a.m. for MONTS-EN-TERNOIS (about 9 miles) & billetted there for the night. G.O.R. arrived from leave. Casualties Nil.	G.H.Q.
NOEUX	6.11.16		Battn. marched off at 9 a.m. for NOEUX (12 miles) & billetted there. Casualties Nil.	G.H.Q.
	7.11.16		Company training. Casualties Nil. No 2685 Sgt G Cartwright & No 4442 L/Cpl D.J Gatzayer awarded D.C.M. 7.11.16	G.H.Q.
	8.11.16		Battery. Casualties Nil.	G.H.Q.
	9.11.16		" Casualties Nil.	G.H.Q.
	10.11.16		" "	G.H.Q.
	11.11.16		" Brigade Staff Parade. Casualties Nil	G.H.Q.
	12.11.16		Instruction to N.C.Os. Church Parade	G.H.Q.
	13.11.16		Company & Specialist Training.	G.H.Q.
	14.11.16		do do	G.H.Q.
AUTHEAU	15.11.16	10.10 a.m	At 10.10 a.m. Bn. left NOEUX and marched to AUTHEAU (10-11 miles) arr. 3.15 p.m. Went into Billets. Casualties Nil.	G.H.Q.
ST. OUEN	16.11.16	9.30 a.m	At 9.30 a.m Bn. left for ST.OUEN (10 mile) arr. 2.45 p.m. Billets for night. Casualties Nil.	G.H.Q.
Near ST PIERRE DIVION	17.11.16	9.30 a.m	At 9.30 a.m. Bn. left in lines. Arr. at HAMEL at 3.15 p.m. attchd to 56th Inf Bgd. 19th Div. Relieves E. Lanc. A & B Coy in support line HANSA Trenches. C & D Coy & H.Q. in German Dug outs captured 13. Casualties Nil.	G.H.Q.
"	18.11.16		A & B Coy relieved E.LANCS in HANSA members. C & B Coy & H.Q. took over support line (HANS) treated by A & B Coy. Casualties. Wounded O.R. 2.	G.H.Q.
"	19.11.16		A & B Coy in HANSA trenches. C & D Coy & H.Q. return to German Dug outs, being relieved in HANSA's support line by E. LANCS. In moving C & D Coys were carrying party for MANCHESTER Pioneer Bn digging new front-line trench. They brought in 3 wounded & 1 unwounded man belonging to 2/6th & 10th Worcesters who had been in shell hole since attacks at 6 a.m. on the	G.H.Q.

1875¹ Wt. W593/826 1,000,000 4/15 J.B.C. & A. A.D.S.S./Forms/C. 2118.

Army Form C. 2118

WAR DIARY
or
INTELLIGENCE SUMMARY
No 2   2/7 Worcestershire Regt
(Erase heading not required.)

Instructions regarding War Diaries and Intelligence Summaries are contained in F.S. Regs., Part II. and the Staff Manual respectively. Title Pages will be prepared in manuscript.

Place	Date	Hour	Summary of Events and Information	Remarks and references to Appendices
Nr ST PIERRE DIVION	19.11.16		Previous day. B Coy lost one man this rifle fire. Casualties Killed O.R. 3 Wounded 2nd Lieut. H.J. PADDISON (slightly at duty) O.R. 8	G/H9
	20.11.16		A & B Coys in HANSA Trenches. C & D Coys & H.Q. in German Dug outs. Casualties wounded O.R. 2	G/H9
AVELUY	21.11.16		Relieved by 9th Batt. SHERWOOD FORESTERS, completed 11.45 p.m. went into Huts at AVELUY. 7 Officers & 2 O.R. joined from Base. Casualties (killed) O.R. 1 wounded O.R. 1.	G/H9
"	22.11.16		At 2.30 p.m. marched to OVILLERS, went into huts. Casualties Nil.	G/H9
OVILLERS	23.11.16		Working Parties. Casualties Nil.	G/H9
"	24.11.16		Working Parties & Specialist-Training. 2nd Lt W.A. BEAMAN & A.C. HANGER join batt. Casualties O.R. 4	G/H9
"	25.11.16		Working Parties & Specialist-Training. Casualties 2/Lt H.J. PADDISON wounded.	G/H9
Nr AVELUY	26.11.16		Batt. left OVILLERS 7 a.m. moved into huts between AVELUY & MARTINSART. Casualties Nil 2	G/H9
	27.11.16		Coy & Specialist-Training. Making Parties in Camp. Casualties Nil 2.	G/H9
	28.11.16		" " " " " " Working Party. Battery Casualties Nil.	G/H9
	29.11.16		Coy & Specialist-Training. Working Parties. Imaging Parties in Camp. Casualties Nil 2.	G/H9
Nr OVILLERS	30.11.16		Batt moved into huts in NAB Road, nr Ovillers. Casualties Nil	G/H9

S.B. Norman Lt.Col.
2/7 Worc'r Regt.

Vol 8

CONFIDENTIAL
WAR DIARY.
2/7 WORCESTERS.
DECEMBER 1916.

Army Form C. 2118.

No 1 WAR DIARY
of
INTELLIGENCE SUMMARY. 2/7 Worc. Regt.
(Erase heading not required.)

Instructions regarding War Diaries and Intelligence Summaries are contained in F. S. Regs., Part II. and the Staff Manual respectively. Title pages will be prepared in manuscript.

Place	Date	Hour	Summary of Events and Information	Remarks and references to Appendices
OVILLERS	1/12/16		Coy & Specialist Training. Working Parties. 2nd Lieut B B Grace rejoined from Base 2/Lt Working Parties. Casualties N12.	
	2.12.16			6/4/5
	3.12.16		Church Parade. Casualties N12	6/4/5
	4.12.16		" Casualties O.R. Died of wounds 2 Wounded 1	6/4/5
MOUQUET FARM	5.12.16		Relieved 2/6 Worc Regt in REGINA & COURCELETTE Trenches. OR Blown water in Sap Casualties Wounded OR.1	
	6.12.16		Left 2/4 Glos. Relief complete 9 p.m. Casualties Wounded O.R.I Trench Routine. Casualties N12	6/4/5
	7.12.16		" " Wounded 5. O.R. 1 (accidentally)	6/4/5
	8.12.16		" " N12	6/4/5
	9.12.16		" 2 men injured from Base Casualties Killed OR 2 Wounded OR 3	6/4/5
"MARTINSART	10.12.16		" & Relief. Relieved by 2/7 R.Warwicks. bugle 11 p.m. Took over huts 5	6/4/5
	11.12.16		w MARTINSART from 2/7 R.Warwicks. Casualties O.R. Killed 1 Wounded 6	
	12.12.16		Cleaning up. Casualties OR wounded S.L.	6/4/5
HEDAUVILLE	13.12.16	10.40 a.m.	B.N. moves off to HEDAUVILLE & took over Billets from 2/8 Bgnt Casualties N12	6/4/5
	14.12.16		Bathing & Training. Casualties N12.	6/4/5
	15.12.16		" "	6/4/5

Training. Casualties N12.

WAR DIARY
INTELLIGENCE SUMMARY — WORCESTERSHIRE REGT.

No 2

Army Form C. 2118.

Place	Date	Hour	Summary of Events and Information	Remarks and references to Appendices
HEDAUVILLE	16.12.16		Training. Casualties NIL.	
	17.12.16		Church Parade " "	
	18.12.16		Training & bathing Casualties NIL	
	19.12.16		" " " "	
	20.12.16		" & working party Casualties NIL	
	21.12.16		" " " "	
MARTINSART	22.12.16		Battn left HEDAUVILLE at 9.30a.m. & marched to MARTINSART. Taking over huts from 2/7 R.Warwicks. Casualties NIL	
	23.12.16		Working parties Casualties NIL	
	24.12.16		" " " wounded O.R.1	
	25.12.16		" " Xmas dinner. Casualties NIL	
	26.12.16		" " Casualties NIL	
	27.12.16		" " " "	
BOUZINCOURT RIGHT SECTOR	28.12.16		Relieved 2/1st Bucks in Regina & Courcelette Trenches. Relief complete 3:30 A.M. 29 Dec. Casualties NIL. On the left 2/6 Glosters. On the right Argyle & Sutherland H'lndrs. Casualties NIL	
	29.12.16		Trench routine. Casualties NIL	
	30.12.16		" " L/c Becket wounded by shrapnel.	
	31.12.16		" " Casualties wounded O.R.1	

Vol 9

War Diary
of
2/7th Batt: The Worcestershire Regt
from
1st to 31st January 1917.

Army Form C. 2118.

WAR DIARY
of
INTELLIGENCE SUMMARY. 2/7 Worcestershire Regt.

No 1

(Erase heading not required.)

Instructions regarding War Diaries and Intelligence Summaries are contained in F.S. Regs., Part II. and the Staff Manual respectively. Title pages will be prepared in 'manuscript.'

Place	Date	Hour	Summary of Events and Information	Remarks and references to Appendices
MOLQUET FARM, RF SECTOR.	1.1.17		Trench relieve. Relieved at night by 2/8 Worc Regt. Relief complete 8.30 p.m. C & D Companies take over, A & B Companies of 2/8 Worcs. Casualties Wounded O.R. 1	9.1.19
WELLINGTON HUTS, NABROAD	2.1.17		Working parties. Casualties Nil	5.1.19
	3.1.17		" I.C.S.M. from Base. Casualties Nil	5.1.19
	4.1.17		" " " " Casualties Nil	5.1.19
	5.1.17		" Draft of 25 men arrived. Casualties Nil	5.1.19
MARTIN-SART.	6.1.17		Batts. Tools and Huts Nr MARTINSART from 2/7 R WARWICKS. C Coy relieved Casualties Nil	5.1.19
	7.1.17		Bathing. D Coy relieved. Short lecture to officers & NCOs by B.G.C. Casualties Nil.	5.1.19
	8.1.17		Bathing & working parties. Casualties Nil. No 2664 Cpl Skelding C.S.M No 3552 Gardner E F awards M.M. Gardner E F awards S.M.M.	5.1.19
	9.1.17		Working Parties "	5.1.19
	10.1.17		" "	5.1.19
	11.1.17		" Draft of 3 men from Base. Casualties Nil	5.1.19
	12.1.17		" " " Casualties Nil	5.1.19
	13.1.17		" " "	5.1.19
	14.1.17		Interior Economy. Coys inspected by C.O. Casualties Nil.	5.1.19
VARENNE	15.1.17		Battn left huts nr MARTINSART 9 a.m. & marched to huts at VARENNES (7 miles) Casualties Nil	5.1.19

Army Form C. 2118.

WAR DIARY

No. 2

INTELLIGENCE SUMMARY. 2/7 Worcestershire Regt.

(Erase heading not required.)

Instructions regarding War Diaries and Intelligence Summaries are contained in F.S. Regs., Part II. and the Staff Manual respectively. Title pages will be prepared in manuscript.

Place	Date	Hour	Summary of Events and Information	Remarks and references to Appendices
VARENNES	16.1.17		Battn. left VARENNES 8.30am marched to BEAUQUESNE (8 miles) In Billets. Casualties NIL	5/Hg.
BEAUQUESNE	17.1.17		Battn. left BEAUQUESNE 9 a.m. marched to HEUZECOURT (15 miles) Thro' the Snow. In billets Casualties NIL	5/Hg.
HEUZECOURT				
AGENVILLE	18.1.17		Left HEUZECOURT 10 a.m. marched to AGENVILLE (4 miles) In Billets. Casualties NIL	5/Hg.
MARCHEVILLE	19.1.17		Left AGENVILLE 8 a.m. marched to MARCHEVILLE (11½ miles). In Billets. Casualties NIL	5/Hg.
			On Bde march from VARENNES no man fell out (38½ miles) mentioned in Div Orders	
	20.1.17		Rei-Inspection Draft 16 S.O.R. arrived from Base Depot. Casualties NIL	5/Hg.
	21.1.17		Church Parade. Casualties NIL. D Coy Transferred to Billets at DONVAST.	5/Hg.
	22.1.17		Bathing. Inlieu Economy. Casualties NIL	5/Hg.
	23.1.17		Bathing. Inspection by C.O. & N.C.O.'s by Training. Casualties NIL	5/Hg.
	24.1.17		Coy Training. 2/Lt. WILSON G.W. & 2/Lt. SOUTHWELL M.G. from Battn. Casualties NIL	5/Hg.
	25.1.17		Coy " 2 O.R. join from 3 Base. Casualties NIL	5/Hg.
	26.1.17		" " Casualties NIL	5/Hg.
	27.1.17		Training. 2/Lieut ROBINSON H.V.G reports in unit. Casualties NIL	5/Hg.
	28.1.17		Church Parade Draft of 8.2 arrive from 4.6 I.B.D. Casualties NIL	5/Hg.
			"B" Coy send 20 S Platoon to CORNEHOTTE for special Training.	
	29.1.17		Training Casualties NIL	5/Hg.
	30.1.17		Training " " " "	5/Hg.
	31.1.17		" "D" Coy take over billets from R.E.s at MARCHEVILLE. Casualties NIL	5/Hg.

L.C. Workman Lieut
2/7 Worc. Regt.

T.134. Wt. W708-776. 500,000. 4/15. Sh. J.C.&S.

Vol 10

February 1917

War Diary
- of -
2/7th Worcester Regt.

Army Form C. 2118.

WAR DIARY
or
INTELLIGENCE SUMMARY.   2/7 WORCESTERSHIRE REGT.

No. 1.

Instructions regarding War Diaries and Intelligence Summaries are contained in F. S. Regs., Part II. and the Staff Manual respectively. Title pages will be prepared in manuscript.

(Erase heading not required.)

Place	Date	Hour	Summary of Events and Information	Remarks and references to Appendices
MARCHEVILLE	1.2.17		Training – Company & Specialist. Casualties NIL.	G.H.Q
"	2.2.17		" – The Attack. "	G.H.Q
"	3.2.17		" " "	G.H.Q
BUSSUS-BUSSUEL	4.2.17		Batt. left MARCHEVILLE at 9.25am & marched to BUSSUS-BUSSUEL (10 mls.). Billeted there. Rec'd notification Capt HANCOCKS (wounded) sick to ENGLAND 26.1.17. Casualties NIL	G.H.Q
	5.2.17		Training – Company & Specialist. Casualties NIL	G.H.Q
	6.2.17		"	G.H.Q
	7.2.17		"	G.H.Q
	8.2.17		"	G.H.Q
	9.2.17		"	G.H.Q
	10.2.17		"	G.H.Q
	11.2.17		Church Parade. Casualties NIL	G.H.Q
	12.2.17		Coy & Spec. Training. Transport left Bussus-Bussuel for new area. 2.O.R. joined from 46 J.B.D. Cas. NIL	G.H.Q
	13.2.17		" " " Cas. NIL	G.H.Q
WIENCOURT	14.2.17		At 11.30am Batt. marched from BUSSUS-BUSSUEL to PONT-REMY & entrained. Detrained at MARCEL CAVE & marched to WIENCOURT arriving 2.15am 15th & billetted. Transport arrived WIENCOURT. Cas. NIL	G.H.Q
	15.2.17		Interior Economy. Cas. NIL	G.H.Q
FRAMERVILLE	16.2.17		Batt. marched to FRAMERVILLE & took over billets. Advance party went into line held by French. Cas. NIL	G.H.Q

T.1144. Wt. W708-776. 500000. 4/15. Sch. J.C.&S.

Army Form C. 2118.

WAR DIARY
or
INTELLIGENCE SUMMARY.

2/7 Worcestershire Regt.

No. 2

(Erase heading not required.)

Place	Date	Hour	Summary of Events and Information	Remarks and references to Appendices
CHAULNES Section.	17.2.17		Batt. relieved 130 Inf Regt (French Army) in centre sub section CHAULNES completing by 3 a.m. 18.2. on the left 2/7 Glos. Regt - 2/8 Worcs A & B found. line C & D support line. Casualties N.F.	S.H.F.
	18.2.17		French Routine Casualties wounded 2 O.R. 1.	S.H.F.
	19.2.17		" Battn. withdrawn from centre sub section & put in reserve dugouts 4 Officers &	S.H.F.
			tended their front & right as far as the PRESSOIRE - CHAULNES Road (inclusive) & joined up north. The 8"Y" ores	S.H.F.
			who extended their left to touch above road - Reliefs completed without incident by 3am 20.2. Cas. Nil	S.H.F.
	20.2.17		Working & Carrying Parties. Casualties NIL	S.H.F.
	21.2.17		" " "	S.H.F.
	22.23.24		" " "	S.H.F.
HARBONNIERES	25.2.17		Relieved by 2/6 Warwicks in Reserve Dugouts & PARISON Dugouts completing by 8:30 p.m. Troops over billets from 2/7 Warwicks at HARBONNIERES. 2nd Lieut Gascoyne B.B. transfered to M.G. Corps. Cas Nil	S.H.F.
	26.2.17		Interior economy. Cas Nil	S.H.F.
	27.2.17		Inspections & battery. Cas Nil	S.H.F.
	28.2.17		Company & Specialist Training. Cas Nil	S.H.F.

26 Feb 17

R. C. Bowman Lt-Col
2/7 Worcs. Rt.

Vol XI.

March 1917

War Diary

of

2/7th Batt. The Worcs Regt.

Army Form C. 2118.

WAR DIARY
of
INTELLIGENCE SUMMARY. 2/7 WORCESTERSHIRE REGT.
(Erase heading not required.)

No 1

Instructions regarding War Diaries and Intelligence Summaries are contained in F. S. Regs., Part II. and the Staff Manual respectively. Title pages will be prepared in manuscript.

Place	Date	Hour	Summary of Events and Information	Remarks and references to Appendices
HARBONNIÈRES	1.3.17		Coy & Specialist Training. Wiring & digging at Night. Bathing. Casualties Nil	S.145
	2.3.17		" " " " " " Casualties Nil	S.145
	3.3.17		Batt'n Training "	S.145
	4.3.17		Church Parade "	S.145
	5.3.17		Coy & Specialist Training "	S.145
	6.3.17		" " " "	S.145
	7.3.17		" " " "	S.145
VAUVILLERS	8.3.17		Batt'n left HARBONNIÈRES at 2.30 p.m. A & B Coys & Advance Party to Trenches KRATZ Section	S.145
			C & D Coys & H.Q. billets at VAUVILLERS. Cas Nil	
CHAULNES Sq	9.3.17		C & D Coys & H.Q. left VAUVILLERS for line KRATZ Sect. Right Sub. Sect. Burning night 9/10th To	S.145
			183rd Inf Bgde. Took Over L1 from A & C O 7 2/7 Worc Regt relieving Hd. 182 H.L.I. completing 11.30 p.m. Cas Nil	
			B & D Coys in Support line A in support. Batt'n on left 2/4 Glouc. Batt'n on right — Cas Nil	S.145
	10.3.17		Trench Routine. Rec'd instructions from W.O. Capt J.D. Simpson urgent for G.S. and to be	
			struck off strength of Batt'n. Casualties Wounded O.R. (L.cpl)	S.145
	11.3.17		Trench Routine. Cas nil. Wounded O.R. 2	S.145
	12.3.17		" H.Dixon J.G., M.C., Lt Cassels W.C. 22nd Hitchin P.D. & 2/Lt.Grosby	S.145
			H.S. joined from Base Depot. Cas Nil	S.145

WAR DIARY

Army Form C. 2118.

No. 2. INTELLIGENCE SUMMARY. 2/7 Worcestershire Regt.

(Erase heading not required.)

Place	Date	Hour	Summary of Events and Information	Remarks and references to Appendices
FRAMERVILLE	13.3.17		Trench Routine. Cas Nil.	
	14.3.17		During night 14/15th Batt relieved by 2/8 Worcs completing 7.45 am 15th.	
			A + D Coys in support at Star Quarries. B & C Coys & H.Q. in billets at FRAMERVILLE. Cas wounded 0R. 1. 5.1/5	
	15.3.17		General cleaning up. Carrying parties. Cas Nil	5.1/5
	16.3.17		Bathing. Interior economy. Cas Nil	5.1/5
	17.3.17		Training. Holiday afternoon. Bgde occupied 1st & 2nd line of German trenches at CHAULNES without opposition. Cas Nil.	5.1/5
Polygon Wood nr CHAULNES	18.3.17		B + C Coys & H.Q. left FRAMERVILLE, A & D Coys left Quarries, moved to dugouts in POLYGON WOOD in front line before CHAULNES. Cas Nil.	5.1/5
C.25.c.7 Map 66D NW	19.3.17		Batt. advanced thro' CHAULNES. H.Q. to C.25.c.7 MAP 66D NW. D Coy to ROUY, B Coy in support at MESNIL ST NICAISE. Batt. of Noels (14th Bgde) on right; A Coy on left front, C in support; 2/6 Glos on left at BETHENCOURT. Cas Nil.	5.1/5
	20.3.17		B Coy relieves D Coy. Patrolling. Working parties. Cas Nil	5.1/5
	21.3.17		Working parties. Cas Nil	5.1/5
	22.3.17		" " making & repairing roads Cas Nil	5.1/5
	23.3.17		Digging strong points & making revetting hurdles.	5.1/5
	24.3.17		Jelbey VILLECOURT Craslin D/Lt CUMBERLAND T.A. joined Battn from Base Dpt. Cas Nil. 5.1/5	

Army Form C. 2118.

WAR DIARY
or
INTELLIGENCE SUMMARY.   2/7 Worcestershire Regt
(Erase heading not required.)

No 3

Place	Date	Hour	Summary of Events and Information	Remarks and references to Appendices
C.2.S.C.2.7. Map.66D.NW to MORCHAIN	25.3.17		Battn. H.Q and B & C Coys moved to MORCHAIN, A Coy remaining at C.28 b. 3.3. Map 66D NW + D Coy going to MORCHAIN MILL. Filling VILLECOURT Cadre gap to 6 p.m. Transport and Q.M's Stores move from FRAMERVILLE to LIHONS. Casualties NIL.	5.H.Q
	26.3.17		Working parties. Battling. 29th Stores NE rejoined from Depôt. Reinforcements O.R. 6 from Base Depôt. Cas. nil.	6.H.Q
	27.3.17		Working parties. Battling. Transport + Q.M Stores move from LIHONS to MORCHAIN. Cas NIL	5.H.Q
MONCHY-LAGACHE	28.3.17		Battling. Battn moved to MONCHY LAGACHE. B & C Coys working parties arriving	5.H.Q
	29.3.17		2/7 WORCS in trailing stony Posts. Cas. NIL.	5.H.Q
			Working Parties & making Billets. Cas. NIL.	7.H.Q
	30.3.17		" " Cas. NIL.	5.H.Q
	31.3.17		" " Battling. Casualties NIL.	5.H.Q

Vol 12

April 1917

War Diary

- of -

2/7th Worcester Regt

Army Form C. 2118.

WAR DIARY
or
INTELLIGENCE SUMMARY.

No. 1   2/7 WORCESTERSHIRE REGT

(Erase heading not required.)

Instructions regarding War Diaries and Intelligence Summaries are contained in F. S. Regs., Part II. and the Staff Manual respectively. Title pages will be prepared in manuscript.

Place	Date	Hour	Summary of Events and Information	Remarks and references to Appendices
VILLEVEQUE to MARTEVILLE	1.4.17		Relieved 2/8 WORCESTERS at VILLEVEQUE; relief complete 11.40 a.m. Capt BOWMAN & party entered and occupied ATTILLY. In the evening the Battn was relieved by the 2/4 GLOUCS. Relief complete at 10.30 p.m. Moved to MARTEVILLE. Casualties NIL	9/4.17
VILLECHOLES	2.4.17		Advanced to VILLECHOLES, HQ arrived 3 p.m. C & D Coys attached to 2/7th MAISSEMY in the afternoon. Casualties O.R. 1 killed 2 wounded.	5/4.17
	3.4.17		General consolidation of posts & work. Casualties O.R. 7 wounded.	
VILLEVEQUE	4.4.17		Relieved at VILLECHOLES by 2/8 WORCESTERS. Relief complete 6.30 p.m. Battn moved to VILLEVEQUE. Casualties O.R. 5 wounded.	5/4.17
	5.4.17		Work on roads & cables in VILLEVEQUE. Casualties NIL.	5/4.17
MARTEVILLE	6.4.17		Relieved 2/4 GLOUCS in MARTEVILLE. Relief complete 11.30 a.m. Casualties NIL.	5/4.17
MONCHY-LAGACHE	7.4.17		2/5 WARWICKS relieved the battn at MARTEVILLE & the batt. returned billets at MONCHY-LAGACHE. Relief complete 12 noon. Casualties NIL	5/4.17
	8.4.17		Bathing, work on craters & roads in vicinity. Casualties NIL	5/4.17
CROIX - MOLIGNAUX	9.4.17		Relieved by 17th Battn ROYAL SCOTS. Went into DIV. REST at CROIX MOLIGNAUX in the after- noon. Casualties NIL Lt. DWAN & Cassels crossposted to 4/7th Battnt. 2/Lts MILBURN & SADLER to 2/7.	5/4.17
	10.4.17		Battn. All Coys worked during the morning on roads in the vicinity of MONCHY-LA-GACHE. All coys worked on roads. Cos NIL.	5/4.17

WAR DIARY

INTELLIGENCE SUMMARY. 2/7 Worcestershire Regt

Army Form C. 2118.

No 2

Place	Date	Hour	Summary of Events and Information	Remarks and references to Appendices
CROIX MOLIG-NAUX	11.4.17		Coys at work on roads. Cas Nil	S.H.R
	12.4.17		" " " Lt Col DORMAN goes to Brigade & has been taken command of Battn. Cas Nil.	S.H.R
	13.4.17		A & D Coys working parties on roads. B & C parade under Coy Cmdrs. C.O's parade of Battn at 6pm. Cas Nil.	S.H.R
	14.4.17		A B & D Coys. " Cadualti Nil. At B Coy battoo. C.O's parade at 6pm.	S.H.R
	15.4.17		A & D Training under Coy Cmdrs. B & C working parties. B Coy brattoo S. C.O's parade 6pm. Cas Nil.	S.H.R
	16.4.17		B & C " " " A & D " " 2-6pm. Med. Insp. Cas Nil.	S.H.R
	17.4.17		A Coy " " " C and B & D " C.O's parade at 8.30 a.m. Cas Nil.	S.H.R
	18.4.17		B & D " " " " A Coy & " " Cas N.12	S.H.R
	19.4.17		C.O's parade at 6.30 am. C & D Coys work on roads 10am to 6pm. At B Coy training. Cas Nil	S.H.R
	20.4.17		C Coy work on roads 10am to 6pm, other Coy training & attack practise. Cas Nil	S.H.R
	21.4.17		Battn. relieved 1/6 Battn LANCS Fus. in GERMAINE. 2 hrs march of two relieved Battn in	S.H.R
GERMAINE			CROIX MOLIGNAUX. All Coys did to by work on roads before march to GERMAINE. Cas Nil.	
	22.4.17		Work on improving & clearing billets. Cas Nil. 9/4 HILL. We proceed to England for special leave.	S.H.R
	23.4.17		" " " A Coy working party at VAUX. C.O's parade 6pm. Cas Nil.	S.H.R
	24.4.17		" " " Battery. C.O's parade 11pm. Inspection of rifles by Army.	S.H.R
	25.4.17		C.O's parade 10-12.30 Clearing up & improving sanitation of billets. 2 Lt DRAKE D B & 2 Lt OR joined from 46 G.B.D. Cas Nil.	S.H.R
		am & pm	Major H Col DORMAN returned from Brigade & reumed command of Battn. Cas Nil. Lt HARRISON & proceeds to R.F.C. 2 observer in aeroplane.	

T.134. Wt. W708 776. 500000 4/15. Sir J.C. & S.

WAR DIARY *or* **INTELLIGENCE SUMMARY**   2/7 Worcestershire Regt.   No 3

Army Form C. 2118.

Place	Date	Hour	Summary of Events and Information	Remarks and references to Appendices
GERMAINE	26.4.17		C.O.'s parade 10-12 a.m. In the afternoon inter Company football matches. Cas: Nil	F/14
	27.4.17		C.O.'s parade 10-1 p.m. In afternoon Batt. Football team played 1/7th Worcesters — drawn game 1:1. Cas Nil	
	28.4.17		C.D & B.Y. Foot bathing & special training. C & D Coys attack practice including use of rifle grenades. A & B Coys training, bombing & musketry. Cas Nil	F/15
	29.4.17		Church parade. C Company party. A Coy practice attack, including use of rifle grenades. B & D Coys smoke bomb drill. Playing football in middle of day. 5.30 p.m. C/46 Platoon Parnall - Shaikim War 2 hrs - Nil. Cas. Nil	F/16
	30.4.17		A B & C Coys Company training. D Coy opened with deflecting ten platoons back for artillery Maneuvers. The G.O.C. Division being present. Col. O.C.	F/16

Battalion Orders No 268 17 March 1917 Italian Decorations

{ No.2675 Sergt CARTWRIGHT G 2/7 Worc Regt } Bronze medal for Military Valour
{ No 4443 L/Cpl BATHERGOOD   "   " }

Div Routine Orders No 1072 29th April 1917   MILITARY MEDAL

MILITARY MEDAL { No 201866 Pte M HART   D Coy 2/7 War. Regt. } Awarded the Military Medal
                { " 207857   "   H CLARKE D Coy   "   }

C.J. Wunnaw Lt Col
2/7 Worc R.

May 1917

War Diary
- of -
2/7th Worcester Regiment

Army Form C. 2118.

WAR DIARY
of
INTELLIGENCE SUMMARY. 2/7 Worcestershire Regt.

No. 1

(Erase heading not required.)

Instructions regarding War Diaries and Intelligence Summaries are contained in F.S. Regs., Part II. and the Staff Manual respectively. Title pages will be prepared in manuscript.

Place	Date	Hour	Summary of Events and Information	Remarks and references to Appendices
GERMAINE	1.5.17		9-10 a.m. Coy under Coy Commanders. 10-11 a.m. C.O's parade. 1-30-3-30 p.m. Inspection of Bgde. by G.O.C. Div. & presentation of Parchment for gallantry in action. Parchments awarded to following men of 2/7 Worc. Regt. No 201503 P.S. CHATER. No 203525 P.S. HARRISON. T.A. No 20169. P.G. NICKLIN H. Cas NIL	G.N.4.
LEFT SUPPORT HOLNON SECTOR	2.5.17		163rd Bde. relieved 182nd Bgde in HOLNON Sector. 2/7 Worc Regt left GERMAINE 4.30 p.m. Relieved 2/5 GLOSTERS in left Support. Taking over completing 10.10 p.m. 2/6 "A" Gloster Coy in Outpost Line. R.E. Support Bn. 2/4 Glos. 2/6 Worcs. in Reserve at ATILLY. 15th SHERWOODS on our left. Lt. MANUEL T (M.O.) reported from Hosp. Capt. WOOD reported TA. Cas NIL	SMS
B.S.17			Trench Routine. Working Parties in BROWN LINE. In evening "A" Patrol of 2/7 Worcs went out from outpost line under 2/Lt CONSTANTINE. SOUTHWELL, SHERLOCK & LAWRENCE respectively and although brilliance of the moon prevented any offensive action by lay parties much useful information was gained. 2/Lt COOK G.M. joined Battn. from Base Dpt. & 2/Lt COOK. Cas NIL	SNS
	4.5.17		Trench Routine. Working parties in BROWN LINE. 9.40 p.m. Patrol of 5 O.R. under Lt BLACKBURN left M.29.07.9.4 moved due East on to the GRICOURT = ST QUENTIN Road. Patrol then moved S.E. about 100 yds. The road being found in good condition except for a few shell holes. At this point the enemy's artillery became heavy fire on our left front & a M.G. began firing over the road. Enemy trench light & continual M.G. fire from the direction of KIRWORTH STICKS the	

T.J. 134. Wt. W708-776. 500,000. 4/15. Sir J. C. & S.

WAR DIARY or INTELLIGENCE SUMMARY.

Army Form C. 2118.

2/7 Worcestershire Regt.

No 2

Place	Date	Hour	Summary of Events and Information	Remarks and references to Appendices
			Patrol was fired on & withdrawn. Cas. Nil.	
	6.9.17		Trench Routine. At 11.5 p.m. Patrol of 1 S.O.R. under Lt BLACKBURNE left the GRICOURT-ST QUENTIN Road in M2.q.d. Patrol divided into 3 parties. Left Party advanced towards the North from KILWORTH STICKS at M30.a.2.1. and reached within 30 yards where they were fired on by the enemy holding the bank to which they moved rapidly replied. Right party then advanced towards the N.W. end of KILWORTH STICKS and also succeeded within 30 yards when a Very light was fired at them & heavy fire opened. A party of the enemy then left the bank & moving N. attempted to outflank an left patrol & fought splendidly fire to bear on it. The third party of the patrol was then supposed to deal with the outflanking movement - but eventually owing to lack of time & enemy being apparently reinforced Lt BLACKBURNE successfully withdrew his patrols back on the Road. Cas. Nil.	S.H.S
Out post Hulch	6/7/17		2/7 Worcs three one coy of 2/6 Worcs attacked relieved 2/6 Glos. John are by 2/4 Glos in the outpost line. Relief was complete without incident by 11.45a.m. 7th. On the left 1/9 D.L.I Relief 1/3/2 Brigade.	
HOLNON SECTOR			Cas. Nil. Received 2 O.R. from Base.	S.H.S
	7.9.17		Patrol of 10 O.R. under Sergt ROBINSON left M2.q.7.5 & moved E arriving the GRICOURT-ST QUENTIN Road & halted when 100 yards from N. end of KILWORTH. Very lights were sent up from both ends of the wood & M.G. opened fire immediately whilst firing in a Northerly direction. Patrol then moved towards the right trench of the wood & from there sounds of whistling were heard (similar to	2HS

WAR DIARY or INTELLIGENCE SUMMARY

2/7 WORCESTERSHIRE Regt.

Army Form C. 2118
No. 111

Place	Date	Hour	Summary of Events and Information	Remarks and references to Appendices
Outpost Line HOLNON SECTOR				
	8.5.17		Relieved by our patrol two nights before. Patrol returned on completing their reconnaissance. Exploration head in CEPY FARM about midnight's. Casualties 9/Lt CONSTANTINE H.S. wounded. 2nd Lt NEAP took out a patrol from S.6 b.4.5 at 10.15 pm for the purpose of examining ground round CEPY FARM. Patrol reached S.6 b.7.2 where it came under rifle fire at very light, fired apparently from ST QUENTIN Road at T.1.c.8. where ground of talking were heard. A belt of wire runs along the North side of the road which prevents further progress. Positions of JORDAN & KILWORTH & BRICOURT - QUENTIN ROAD and approaches to it were about 75% of it. N.W. end of KILWORTH STICKS are a reconnoitring patrol. Very lights were sent up at regular intervals & a M.G. pitched apparently immediately to the E. of The Copse fired several bursts up the valley in a N. direction. 1 O.R. who lay out as a listening post within 30 yards of the N.W. portal of CEPY FARM at 10.30 pm who opened hundred yds of a sniper locality his rifle had no copies of the enemy working meanwhile. At 11.45 pm there were two men exploring at CEPY FARM. Casualties. Cas. Killed O.R. 1. wounded O.R. 2. Patrols 2/Lt HANGER & party LAP. S.6.c 8.3 & reconnoitred Towards BRICOURT QUENTIN RD. where it is sunken about T.1.c.30. A certain amount of random company was put out & barricaded Gap to St QUENTIN Rd. A patrol of 2nd Lt BEAMAN & party report. The enemy apparently using N.of road about S.6. a.9.7 & used off bombing trench from the direction of T.1.c.6.7. Scout HARRIS & small party present the old German line near the O. Pat. M.36.20 & examined a plant distance beyond as a listening post at 11.6 m Very lights were fired from S. of	S.M.S.

WAR DIARY
or
INTELLIGENCE SUMMARY.   2/7 WORCESTERSHIRE REGT

Army Form C. 2118.

No. IV

(Erase heading not required.)

Place	Date	Hour	Summary of Events and Information	Remarks and references to Appendices
OUTPOSTLINE HOLNON SECTOR			CURATE'S CORPSE and a few rifle phot. traffic could be heard on road. To & from Germany lines. Sounds of Glass explosions lights with falling debris were heard at 10 p.m. & twice again at 10.15 p.m. from S of ST. QUENTIN. Sound of transport in the town were louder than on any previous night, ceasing soon after midnight. Cas. Wounded O.R. 1. S.O.S.	
ATTILLY	10.5.17		Relieved by 2/4 Glouces. battn. unrelief went into Bde reserve at ATTILLY 3.45.	S.H.S.
	11.5.17		WALL W. joined from Base Depot. Cas. Nil.	S.H.S.
	12.5.17		Inter-Company Working Parties on BROWN LINE & front-line Trenches. Cas. Nil.	S.H.S.
			Battn Working Parties on 2nd Line & Brown Line Trenches. 2/4 Stokers attached & employed CEPY FARM. D.Coy 2/7 Worc Regt being attached to 143rd & taking over their Right Coy's front line for the attack. Cas Nil.	S.H.S.
	13.5.17		Working parties on Brown Line & front Line Trenches HOLNON SECTOR. Church Parade 6 p.m. Cas. Killed O.R. 1 (acid) 2/Lt CONSTANTINE H.S. died at 3/1st C.C.S. from wounds re- -ceived 7.5.17	S.H.S.
	14.5.17		Working Parties on BROWN LINE & FRONT LINE TRENCHES, HOLNON SECTOR Cas. Nil.	S.H.S.
GERMAINE	15.5.17		163rd B'gde relieved by Reserve 139th Regt in HOLNON sector 2/7 Worcs left ATTILLY 5.30 p.m. marched to GERMAINE & billeted there. Cas Nil.	S.H.S.
	16.5.17		Preparations for move to LONGUEAU area. Cas nil	S.H.S.

WAR DIARY or INTELLIGENCE SUMMARY

Army Form C. 2118

WORCESTERSHIRE REGT

Nov

Place	Date	Hour	Summary of Events and Information	Remarks and references to Appendices
HERLY	17.5.17		At 11 a.m. Battn marched off from GERMAINE & arrived at HERLY (near NESTLE) at 10.30 a.m. 11 miles (Transport escort) Cas. Nil	S.H.
VILLERS-BOCAGE	18.5.17	at 7.15 a.m.	Battn left HERLY & marched to NESTLE STN. Entrained. Train left at 9.15 a.m. Detrained at AMIENS, marched to VILLERS BOCAGE (11 miles) arriving 4 p.m. & billetted. Remained left HERLY at 10 a.m. & travelled via NESLE & WARVILLERS. 9.H.B. Cas. Nil.	S.H.
	19.5.17		Interior economy. Transport travelled via QUESNEL to DOMART Cas. Nil	S.H.
	20.5.17		Church Parade. Transport travelled via AMIENS to VILLERS BOCAGE. Cas. Nil	S.H.
BEAUVAL	21.5.17	at 7.30 a.m.	Battn left VILLERS BOCAGE & marched to BEAUVAL (8 miles) arriving 10.40 a.m. Afternoon bathing. Cas. Nil	S.H.
	22.5.17		Bathing. Cas. Nil	S.H.
SUS-ST LEGER	23.5.17	at 7 a.m.	Battn left BEAUVAL marched to SUS-ST LEGER (12 miles) arrived noon & billetted. Cas. Nil	S.H.
DAINVILLE	24.5.17	At 9.18 a.m.	Battn left SUS-ST LEGER & with Brigade marched to REBAC DU SUD (9 miles) & entrained, arrived DAINVILLE nr ARRAS 3.0 p.m. Battn accommodated in farm & Mays. Nahments & under canvas at L.18.a. The grt arrived at 4.30 p.m. Received on Reg'Platers - Lt Col DORMAN L.C. Capt Thompson G.A. Lt & Q.M. CLEMO F.J.; Cy S.M. GRIFFITHS, H. Cas. Nil	S.H.
	25.5.17		Rest & cleaning up. Cas Nil	S.H.

WAR DIARY

INTELLIGENCE SUMMARY. 2/7 Worcestershire Regt.

Army Form C. 2118.

N° VI

Place	Date	Hour	Summary of Events and Information	Remarks and references to Appendices
DAINVILLE	26.5.17		Training. Casualties whilst practising the attack, a man of A Coy accidentally trod on a dead HALE'S GRENADE lying in the long grass & it exploded wounding 11 O.R.	S.O.S.
	27.5.17		Church Parade. Training. Surrender of B Coy. Cas N.i.L.	S.O.S
	28.5.17		Training. Bomb Off D Coy (2nd Lieut. K—) O.R 1 (accd) Wounded 2/L DORE— HILL W.T. & O.R. 2 (accd) All at Bn Bombing School a Mills Hand Grenade prematurely exploding.	S.O.S.
	29.5.17		Practise of the Battn in the attack as part of General 1st Line Trenches (Map 51B.S.W. M19d & M20c) held by C. who were present. A & D Coys (right + left) 1st & 2nd attacking waves. + B & C Coys(right + left) 3rd + 4th waves. Surrendered 9 A + C Coys. Cas Nil	S.O.S
	30.5.17		Coy Training. Trench Demonstration for Officers at WAILLY. Night Outpost practice. Cas N.i.L.	S.O.S
	31.5.17		Coy Training A, B + C Coys. String on Range D Coy. Revolver practice for Officers. Cas N.i.L.	S.O.S

E. Alveen Major
O.C 2/7 Worcestershire Regt.

Vol 14

June 1917.

War Diary

of

2/7th Battn Worcestershire Regt

Army Form C. 2118.

WAR DIARY
or
INTELLIGENCE SUMMARY.   2/7 WORCESTERSHIRE REGT.

No 1

(Erase heading not required.)

Instructions regarding War Diaries and Intelligence Summaries are contained in F.S. Regs., Part II. and the Staff Manual respectively. Title pages will be prepared in manuscript.

Place	Date	Hour	Summary of Events and Information	Remarks and references to Appendices
TILLOY	1-6-17		2/7th Batt Worc Regt relieved 2/1st Batt Bucks in support at TILLOY-Lez-MOFFLAINES. Complete 11:30 P.M. Cas. Nil.	9/145.
	2.6.17		Working parties on C.T's by night. Lt Col. DORMAN awarded D.S.O. R.S.M. ABRAHAMS the M.S.M. Cas. all Nil.	9/145.
	3.6.17		" " " Cas. DR. 1 Killed 4 wounded.	9/145.
	4.6.17		" " " Cas. Nil.	5/145.
	5.6.17		" " " Work stopped by gas shelling. Lt Col Dorman returned from leave. Bathing. Cas. Nil. 2nd Lt DOREHILL WJ. transferred to ENGLAND wounded	5/145.
	6.6.17		Working Parties on C.T's to by night. Cas. Nil.	5/145.
	7.6.17		Training 5 A.M. to 10 A.M. & 5 P.M. to 7 P.M. Boy 2 to 4 pm en rouge. Cas. Nil.	5/145.
	8.6.17		" " Cas. O.R. wounded attached to R.E. Tunnelling Coy.	5/145.
	9.6.17		8 A.M. to 12 A.M. & 5 P.M. to 6 P.M. Cas. Nil.	5/145.
SIMENCOURT	10.6.17		Bathing during day. At 7 P.M. Bn left TILLOY & marched to SIMENCOURT (8½ miles). Arrived 11:15 P.M. Q.M.s Stores & Transport also move to SIMENCOURT. Took over B.H. Huts etc from LONDON SCOTTISH. Cas Nil.	5/145.
	11.6.17		Rest. Cleaning up. Kit Inspections. Bathing. Cas. Nil.	5/145.
	12.6.17		" " " Cas. Nil.	5/145.
	13.6.17		Training & Recreation. Bathing	9/145.
	14.6.17		" "	9/145.

Battalion Training.

Army Form C. 2118.

WAR DIARY
of
INTELLIGENCE SUMMARY. 2/7 WORCESTERSHIRE REGT
(Erase heading not required.)

No 2

Instructions regarding War Diaries and Intelligence Summaries are contained in F.S. Regs., Part II. and the Staff Manual respectively. Title pages will be prepared in manuscript.

Place	Date	Hour	Summary of Events and Information	Remarks and references to Appendices
SIMENCOURT	15.6.17		Training & Recreation. Cas. Nil.	G.H.Q.
"	16.6.17		"	G.H.Q.
"	17.6.17		Church parade. Brigade Sports. Battn won 2 out of 9 events & was 1st in Officers tug of war heat. Cas. Nil.	G.H.Q.
	18.6.17		Training. Cas. Nil.	G.H.Q.
	19.6.17		Inspection by B.G.C. of Battalion billets, cookhouses, Q.M's stores & Transport. Deficiencies in equipment. Cas. Nil.	G.H.Q.
	20.6.17		Holiday. Brigade Sports. Cas. nil.	G.H.Q.
	21.6.17		Training. Transport departs at 4 p.m. for new area. Cas. nil.	G.H.Q.
	22.6.17		Battn leaves SIMENCOURT at 8.45 a.m.; marched to GOUY-EN-ARTOIS & entrained at 11 a.m. Detrained at HESDIN at 5 p.m.; marched to VIEIL HESDIN & billetted there. Transport arrived 2.30 p.m. Cas. Nil.	G.H.Q.
	23.6.17		Inspⁿ made by Commandies. Cas Nil.	G.H.Q.
	24.6.17		Church Parade. Cas. Nil.	G.H.Q.
	25.6.17		Coy & Battn training. Battn exercise for Officers. Cas. nil. OR 3 joined from 26 IBD.	G.H.Q.
	26&27.6.17		Training. Cas Nil.	G.H.Q.
	28.6.17		Training. Casualties. Wounded OR 1 (accidentally) at Bombs of the Rifle Grenade Class.	G.H.Q.
	29.6.17		" Cas Nil	G.H.Q.
	30.6.17		Holiday. Battn Sports. Marshall Sports & Horse Shows. Cas nil.	G.H.Q.

L. E. Lahman Lt Col
2/7 Wor C. R.

2/7TH WORCESTERS

Vol 15

WAR DIARY

JULY 1917.

Army Form C. 2118.

WAR DIARY
or
INTELLIGENCE SUMMARY.
(Erase heading not required.)

No. 1 2/7 WORCESTERSHIRE REGIMENT

Place	Date	Hour	Summary of Events and Information	Remarks and references to Appendices
VIEIL HESDIN	July 1917 1-7-17		Presentation of ribands + parchments to 183rd B/de by G.O.C Division. Recipients from 2/7th WORCESTERSHIRE REGIMENT	
			200736 L/Sgt SKELDING C.S. Military Medal	
			201223 Pte GARDNER E.F. ditto	
			201887 Pte CLARKE F. ditto	
			203311 Pte CORBETT C. Div. Commander's Parchment. Cas. Nil	5/H5
	2-3-4-5/7/17		Training. Cas Nil	5/H5
	6.7.17		Training. Batln Platoon Competition: Winners No 14 Platoon D Coy. Reinforcements O.R. 2 from H6th I.B.D. Cas Nil	5/H5
	7.7.17		Training. B/de Scheme. Cas Nil	5/H5
	8.7.17		Church Parade — Cas Nil.	5/H5
	9.7.17		Training. D Coy compete in B/de Inter Coy Competition. No 14 Platoon of D Coy compete in Inter Platoon Competition + won the Brigade Competition. Cas. Nil	5/H5
	10.7.17		Training. DIV. H.Q Sports No 14 Platoon D Coy in Th Div Platoon Competition Represents 183 B/de. Recall 1st C.Q.M.S. Entrances 20763 B/de. 2 2/7 "Warwicks" 20712 B/de. 3 2/7 Worcs. 20783 B/de. O.R. 14 Transferred to 40257 Employment Coy Labour Corps Cas.Nil	5/H5
	11.7.17		Training. 2/Lt HUTCHINSON A N reported for duty (from 7 Cas Battn Worc. Rt.) Cas . Nil	5/H5
	12.7.17		Training. Cas. Nil	5/H5
	13.7.17		Training. Party of O.R. 30 attached to Central Purchase Board. Cas. Nil	5/H5

WAR DIARY
INTELLIGENCE SUMMARY. WORCESTERSHIRE REGT

Army Form C. 2118.

No 2

(Erase heading not required.)

Instructions regarding War Diaries and Intelligence Summaries are contained in F.S. Regs., Part II. and the Staff Manual respectively. Title pages will be prepared in manuscript.

Place	Date	Hour	Summary of Events and Information	Remarks and references to Appendices
VIEILLE ESDIN	14.7.17		Training. Draft of O.R. 55 joined (Trans. from 8th SUFFOLKS) Cas. Nil.	4. M.G.
	15.7.17		Church Parade. Lt GOODWIN H & 2 Lt HEMINGWAY R.S. report from ENGLAND (Previously evac. sick) O.R. 4 joined from 46th I.B.D. Cas.Nil.	5. M.S
	16-17/7/17		Training. Cas.Nil.	5 M.G.
	18.7.17		Training. Div. Race meeting. 2/Lt FLINT W.m. GALAHMETZ. Gallop on SNIDER Cas. Nil.	5.M.G
	19.7.17		Training. Capt BOUCHER W.E. reported from Div. Dpt Batt. Cas. Nil.	5 H.G
	20.7.17		Training. 2/Lt Robinson H.V.G. apptd Battn Bombing Officer. Cas. Nil.	5.M.G.
	21.7.17		Training. 2/Lt CUMBERLAND J.A. rejoined from Hospital. 2/Lt WHEELER G.W.B. reported for duty. Reinforcements 2 R.1 + O.R. 2 (one pack) report from 46th I.B.D. Cas Nil.	5.M.G.
	22.7.17		Church Parade. – Cas. Nil	4.M.G
	23.7.17		Training. Cas. Nil.	4.M.G
FLERS	24.7.17		Battn left VIEILLE ESDIN at 7.30 a.m. + marched to FLERS. (7½ miles) + billetted there. Cas. nil.	5.M.G.
	25.7.17		Training. Party of 90 from A Coy marched to PETIT HOUVIN for entraining party. Cap 7.15	M.G
ERINGHEM	26.7.17		Battn with drums & Transport marched to PETIT HOUVIN + entrained to ESQUEBECQ, where it detrained + marched to ERINGHEM + billetted. Cas Nil.	2.M.G
	27.7.17		Training. Draft of O.R. 101 arrived midnight 27/28th. Cas. Nil.	4.M.G
	28.7.17		"	4.M.G

Army Form C. 2118.

WAR DIARY
or
INTELLIGENCE SUMMARY.   2/7 WORCESTERSHIRE REGT.

No 3

(Erase heading not required.)

Instructions regarding War Diaries and Intelligence
Summaries are contained in F. S. Regs., Part II.
and the Staff Manual respectively. Title pages
will be prepared in manuscript.

Place	Date	Hour	Summary of Events and Information	Remarks and references to Appendices
ERINGHEM	29.7.17		Church Parade. 2/Lt WATSON A.R. & O.R 2 joined from Reserve Base. Cas- ualties NIL.	5/115
	30.7.17		Training. Cas N/L	5/115
	31.7.17		" "	5/115

F.C. Norman Lt Col
Comdg 2/7 worc. Ry.t

Vol 16

August 1917

War Diary
of
2/7th Bn. The Worcestershire Regt

WAR DIARY

Army Form C. 2118.

Instructions regarding War Diaries and Intelligence Summaries are contained in F. S. Regs., Part II. and the Staff Manual respectively. Title pages will be prepared in manuscript.

No. 1

~~INTELLIGENCE SUMMARY~~

(Erase heading not required.)

2/7 WORCESTERSHIRE REGT.

Place	Date	Hour	Summary of Events and Information	Remarks and references to Appendices
ERINGHEM	1.5.17		Training. Casualties Nil	
	2.5.17		Training Casualties Nil	
	3.5.17		Training Casualties Nil	
	4.5.17		Training Casualties Nil	
	5.5.17		Church Parade. Maj. Green G.H. leaves Battn & proceeds to England. Casualties Nil	
	6.5.17		Training. Capt Rowe A.F. (2/7 Worcester Regt) appointed 2nd in Command, vice Maj. GREEN	
			Reinforcements O.R. 3 from 4th I.B.D. Casualties Nil	
	7.5.17		Brigade Scheme attack practice. Casualties Nil	
	8.5.17		Training. Casualties Nil	
	9.5.17		Training. Casualties Nil	
	10 " "		Training Casualties Nil	
	11 " "		Training Casualties Nil	
	12 " "		Church Parade. Casualties Nil	Casualties Nil
	13 " "		Training. Capt BOUCHER R&E 1/AT HITCHIN P.D. 2/7 CUMBERLAND J.A. WENT 6/7th DEPOT Battn	
	14 " "		Preparing for MOVE. Casualties Nil	

WAR DIARY
INTELLIGENCE SUMMARY. 2/7 Bn Worc. Regt.

Army Form C. 2118.

Place	Date	Hour	Summary of Events and Information	Remarks and references to Appendices
POPERINGHE	15.8.17		at 9.40 a.m. The Batt. left ERINGHEM, marched to ESQUELBECQ and entrained, detrained at HOUTOUTRE station POPERINGHE. Stayed at Camp nr POPERINGHE map ref BELGIUM Sheet 28 N.W. G 9 a 2.6. Transport proceeded to next area by road. Casualties Nil	
YPRES	16.		Marched to GOLDFISH CAMP N. YPRES. map ref. BELGIUM Sheet 28 N.W. HILL C.59. Casualties Nil	
"	17		Prepared to move up to French. moved up to support Troops WIELTJE, in evening relieved 1/1 Worc Rgt Right Support. C.O's horse killed under him. Casualties wounded OR 2.	
"	18		Trench Routine. Transport ammo and rat party (10 all ranks) under Capt N. C. H 7 & 35.3 Sheet 28 N.W. Casualties killed OR 3 wounded OR 9 Died from wounds OR 1	
"	19.		Trench Routine. carrying parties. Casualties Killed OR 3. Wounded OR 26 (2 at duty) OR 1 wounded & Died 19th	
"	20		Batn relieved by 2/1 Bucks Battn OBLI. moved to Goldfish Chateau Camp. Hill C.59. Casualties wounded OR 3 (1 at duty)	
"	21.		Cleaning up etc. Casualties Nil	

WAR DIARY

Army Form C. 2118.

INTELLIGENCE SUMMARY. 1/7 Bn 3/RC Regt.

No. III

(Erase heading not required.)

Place	Date	Hour	Summary of Events and Information	Remarks and references to Appendices
WIELTJE YPRES	22.5.17		Battn moved up to SUPPORT Trenches WIELTJE. Casualties NIL.	
"	23.		Battn relieved 2/1 Buckn Battn in RIGHT FRONT Battn WIELTJE Sector. Casualties. Wounded OR. 9 OR 1 SIW.	
"	24.		HELD LINE. Encountered over 1/Lt LAWRENCE T.A proceeds to ENGLAND for Medical Exam at 150 re Commission in INDIAN army. Casualties Killed OR 1. Wounded OR 11. OR 1 died from Wounds 1/Pietron B by attacks Aisne House (attack unsuccessful)	
"	25.	11 P.M.	1 Platn A Coy under 2/Lt WHALE took AISNE HOUSE but were driven out. 2/Lt WHALE ORGANISING. Casualties Killed OR 3 Wounded Lieut. BLACKBURN GM, 2/Lt HUTCHINSON AN, 9 OR. OR 1 diid from wounds. 2/Lt SADLER C.M. joind 1/3 L.T. M. R.	
"	26.		Relieved in front line by 1/5 Bn Worc Regt. Battn kept in CLOSE SUPPORT. Casualties wounded OR 2. OR 1/4 10/7 min L D. 2 Missing killed. 1. OR.	
"	27.		Brigade attacked. (it was a failure). We relieved part of 2/5 Worc Regt in front line. 2 patrols went out under 2/Lt COOK + BEAMAN. Casualties killed 2/L COOK C.M. + shellfire Casualties OR 20.	
" (contd)	28.		Relieved part of 1/5 WORC Regt. 2/Lt GREEN F.L. proceeds to 46 IBD Etaples an instructor. Casualties followed 2/ OR 2 (Wounds)	

Army Form C. 2118.

WAR DIARY
or
INTELLIGENCE SUMMARY. 2/7 Bn Worc Regt.

No IV

(Erase heading not required.)

Instructions regarding War Diaries and Intelligence Summaries are contained in F. S. Regs., Part II. and the Staff Manual respectively. Title pages will be prepared in manuscript.

Place	Date	Hour	Summary of Events and Information	Remarks and references to Appendices
WIELTJE	29.8.17		Relieved by 2/8 Worc Regt in line, returning to SUPPORT Trenches WIELTJE. Casualties O.R. Killed 3. O.R. wounded 5.	
VLAMERTINGHE	30		Relieved in SUPPORT Trenches by 2/5 R. Warwick. Regt. & came to Red Rose Camp. VLAMERTINGHE. Casualties O.R. 3.	
"	31		Cleaning up. Casualties Nil.	

A. V. Cuss Major
for
O.C. 2/7 Bn Worcestershire Regt.

September 1917

War Diary
of
2/7th & 1/5th The Worcestershire Regt.

Army Form C. 2118.

WAR DIARY
or
INTELLIGENCE SUMMARY.
(Erase heading not required.)

of the 2/7 BATT^N WORCESTERSHIRE REG^T (T.F.)

Instructions regarding War Diaries and Intelligence Summaries are contained in F.S. Regs. Part II. and the Staff Manual respectively. Title pages will be prepared in manuscript.

Place	Date	Hour	Summary of Events and Information	Remarks and references to Appendices
ST. MARTINS	1.9.17		Bn at RED ROSE CAMP. Reorganisation of Companies. 2/LT WOOLDRIDGE appointed Assistant Adjt. Casualties – NIL	
"	2.9.17	10 a.m	Church Parade. 2/LT WATSON.A.E. transferred to 1/8 Bn WORC'S REGT – Casualties – NIL	
"	3.9.17		Training. 2/LT SWANSON J.L. seconded for duty as Gas Officer N° 72. P.O.W. Coy 2/LT CUMBERLAND J.A. rejoined from 61st Div. Depot Bn – Casualties – NIL	
"	4.9.17		Training – Camp visited by G.O.C 61st Divⁿ – Casualties – NIL	
"	5.9.17		Training – 2/LT JORDAN.R. rejoined from Hosp^l – Casualties – NIL	
"	6.9.17		Training – Casualties – wounded O.R.1	
"	7.9.17	7 p.m	Bn proceeded to billets in YSER canal bank N° YPRES – Party to Y3d Base Camp. Casualties. NIL	
CANAL BANK	8.9.17	11-40 p.m	Bn proceeded to front line near POND FARM and relieved 2/7/8? ROYAL WARWICKSHIRE REGT B + C Coys in front line – A + D in support – Casualties – NIL – Bn attached to 184 BDE f^m infant hrs p^g two	
IN THE LINE. E of YPRES	9.9.17		Battⁿ H.Q. shelled from 10.30 a.m. to 5 p.m – Galleries badly damaged. Casualties Killed. O.R.3. Wounded O.R. 11 (including R.S.M.) Artillery Liason Officer killed Bn H Q moved to CAPRICORN KEEP	
"	10.9.17		Under Bn relief at night. A + D in front line + B + C C^{ys} in support. Casualties – wounded O.R.8	
"	11.9.17		Bn relieved at night by 2/6 GLOSTERS – Bn moved into support – Relief complete 3-30 a.m. 12/9/17 Casualties – wounded O.R.5. Gassed CAPT. W.F. SMELLIE. 2/LT GADSBY M.S. + O.R. 28 – 2/LT TWIST W.N. to Hospital.	
"	12.9.17		Working parties in CALL RESERVE TRENCH + dug outs in old German line – Carrying parties at night. Casualties. NIL	
"	13.9.17		D° D° Casualties. NIL	

(A7093). W^t W12839/M1293 75,000. 1/17. D. D. & L., Ltd. Forms/C.2118/14.

WAR DIARY
INTELLIGENCE SUMMARY

of the 2/7th Batt'n WORCESTERSHIRE REG'T (T.F.)

Army Form C. 2118.

Place	Date	Hour	Summary of Events and Information	Remarks and references to Appendices
IN THE LINE E. of YPRES	14/9/17		Batt'n H.Q's in CALL RESERVE taken over by LIVERPOOL SCOTTISH (55th DIVN) as front line 18th H.Q's. Batt'n moved back to bivouacs at PLAMERTINGHE at night. Casualties – NIL	
PLAMERTINGHE	15/9/17		Batt'n paraded by motor buses to YALLEY CAMP-WATOU. CAPT W.E. BOUCHER & 2/LT P.D. HITCHIN rejoined from 61st Divn. Depot 1st. 2/LT F.C. MANGER reported from Temp'y Area Command YPRES N. AREA & HON'le T. COATES, 2/6 B'n BLACK WATCH posted to this B'n. Casualties – NIL	
WATOU	16/9/17		Church Parade. AWARDS - Military Medals - 201443 Pte T. ASHMAN, 203505 A/Sgt. M. DAVIES - 201860 A/Sgt. W. ANDREWS - 201916 Pte W.H. MAPP - 201632 Pte J. LESTER. Casualties – NIL	
"	17/9/17	9.30 am	Batt't marched to billets near WORMHOUDT. Batt't ceased to be att'd to 184th Bde. CAPT W.F. SMELLIE evacuated to ENGLAND (gassed). Casualties – NIL	
WORMHOUDT	18/9/17	8.30 am	Batt't marched to CASSEL ST'N. DAHINCHOVE and entrained. Casualties – NIL	
ARRAS	19/9/17	7.30 am	Batt't detrained at ARRAS and marched to huttments at SIMENCOURT arriving 10.45 a.m. Casualties – NIL. AWARD. MILITARY CROSS – 2/LT BEAMAN	
SIMENCOURT	20/9/17		Training. Bath. Casualties – NIL	
"	21/9/17		Inspection & lecture by Y BRIG. GEN'l 183 Bde. CAPT W.E. BOUCHER & 2/LT P.D. HITCHIN to Divn'l Depot 1st. Casualties – NIL	
"	22/9/17		Cleaning – Casualties – NIL	
"	23/9/17		Church parade. Batt'n marched to LICHFIELD CAMP ST NICHOLAS. ARRAS took over from 2/4 R. WARWICKS. Casualties – NIL – 2/LT F.C. MANGER to Divn.	
ARRAS	24/9/17	8.30 pm	Batt'n relieved 4th 13th YORKSHIRE REG'T. night support 182 Regt. Sub sector GREENLAND HILL SECTOR - Casualties – NIL	
GREENLAND HILL	25/9/17		Trench Routine. Working Parties. Casualties – NIL	
"	26/9/17		D° D° Casualties – NIL	

Army Form C. 2118.

WAR DIARY
or
INTELLIGENCE SUMMARY.
(Erase heading not required.) of the 2/7 Battn WORCESTERSHIRE REGT (T.F.)

Place	Date	Hour	Summary of Events and Information	Remarks and references to Appendices
GREENLAND HILL	27/9/17		Trench Routine – Working parties – Casualties – Nil	
"	28/9/17		Trench Routine – Working parties – Casualties – Nil	
"	29/9/17		Trench Routine – Working parties – Casualties – Nil	
"	30/9/17		Trench Routine – Batt'n relieved 2/6 WORCS in right subsector of Left Brigade Relief completed at 9.30 p.m. without incident – Casualties – Nil	

A.V. Rosefain
Comdg 2/7 Worcesters.

October 1917.

War Diary

of

2/7th Batt'n The Worcestershire Reg't

Vol 18

Army Form C. 2113.

WAR DIARY
INTELLIGENCE SUMMARY.
(Erase heading not required.) 2/7 Bn WORCESTERSHIRE REGT (T.F.)

Place	Date	Hour	Summary of Events and Information	Remarks and references to Appendices
GREENLAND HILL ARRAS	1-10-17		Trench Routine. 2/Lt WHALE J reported P.O.W. (unwounded). 2/Lt BOWMAN A.H. to be acting Captain (additional) 27-8-17 and to command D Coy. Casualties Lid O.R. 1	
	2-10-17		Trench Routine. Casualties. Killed O.R.1 Wounded O.R.2	
	3-10-17		Trench Routine. 2/Lt GREEN F.L. reported from A.G. I.B Depôt (Rouen). 2/Lt WEST W.N. granted 21 days sick leave. Casualties W.2 O.R.4	
	4-10-17		Trench Routine. No. 201316 Pte JONES F.R. (D.Coy) awarded parchment by G.O.C. 61st Division for gallantry. Relieved in Right Sub Sector of sypsector by 2/6 Bn OXFORD & BUCKS L.I. (184 Bde) without incident & proceeded to LICHFIELD Camp ST NICHOLAS. Casualties NIL	
ST NICHOLAS ARRAS	5-10-17		Clearing up & reorganisation. 2/Lt HUTCHINSON. A.N. reported from hospital (21-23-8-17) Casualties. NIL	
	6-10-17		Company Training. Working party at LEWIS BARRACKS. 2/Lt ROBINSON J.H. to Hosp I vick Casualties. NIL	
	7-10-17		Church Parade. Working parties at LEWIS BARRACKS & CANTEEN dump. Casualties NIL	
	8-10-17		Working parties. Casualties NIL	
	9-10-17		" " "	
	10-10-17		" " "	
	11-10-17		" " "	
	12-10-17		" " "	
	13-10-17		" " " . 2/Lt STONE M.C. to Hosp sick, Lt COATS.T adjt & to	
	14-10-17		61st Rein Signal Sch. O/C & R Coy 2/Lts B A.I.M.E. Church Parade. Working Parties. Casualties NIL	

Army Form C. 2118.

WAR DIARY
or
INTELLIGENCE SUMMARY.
(Erase heading not required.) 2/7 Bn WORCESTERSHIRE REGT (T.F.)

Instructions regarding War Diaries and Intelligence Summaries are contained in F.S. Regs., Part II. and the Staff Manual respectively. Title pages will be prepared in manuscript.

Place	Date	Hour	Summary of Events and Information	Remarks and references to Appendices
ST NICHOLAS ARRAS	15.10.17		Working parties. O.R. 5 att'd 183 L.T.M.B	
FAMPOUX	16.10.17	7.20 p.m	Relieved 2/6 R.W. WARWICKS at Right support. CHEMICAL WORKS sect. A & D Coy's + H.Q. in REDDING trench. B Coy in FAMPOUX. C Coy at SINGLE ARCH. Casualties NIL	
	17.10.17		Trench Routine - Working parties. Casualties NIL	
	18.10.17		do. Casualties NIL. 2/Lt Col. DORMAN ceased to command. MAJOR ROWE A.V. assumed command. CAPT BIGWOOD M.S. took duties as record in command. LT BLACKBURNE S. Captain'd 'B' Coy. Casualties NIL	
	19.10.17		Trench Routine - Working parties - Casualties NIL	
	20.10.17		do. Cas. NIL. 2/Lt BOWMAN A H. attd L's Adjt. Last of Captain Com'd 31st Coy 12-9-17. LT BLACKBURNE G.M.I. Att'd Adjt Capt (acting)	
	21.10.17		27-9-17. Casualties NIL	
	22.10.17		Trench Routine - Working parties - Casualties NIL	
	23.10.17		Relieved 2/6-7/8 WORCESTERS in front line night entrance to CHEMICAL WORKS sector. Casualties - NIL	
	24.10.17		Trench Routine - Casualties Killed O.R. 2, Wounded O.R. 2 & C.S.M.Y	
		at 2.30 pm CAPT GOODWIN H.M. 2/LT ROBINSON H.W.G. and 10 oth ranks raided the enemy trenches immediately south of the railway cutting. Casualties killed 2 O.R. Missing 2/LT ROBINSON H.W.G. and O.R. 4. Wounded O.R. 11. Oth. Casualties Killed	See Appendix att. of wounded 7 + 15
	25.10.17		O.R. 2, Wounded O.R. 6	
			Trench Routine - Casualties NIL	
	26.10.17		Trench Routine - Casualties Wounded O.R. 1	

Army Form C. 2118.

WAR DIARY
or
INTELLIGENCE SUMMARY.

(Erase heading not required.) 2/7 Bn WORCESTERSHIRE REGT (T.F.)

Instructions regarding War Diaries and Intelligence Summaries are contained in F. S. Regs., Part II. and the Staff Manual respectively. Title pages will be prepared in manuscript.

Place	Date	Hour	Summary of Events and Information	Remarks and references to Appendices
FAMPOUX	27.10.17		Trench Routine. Casualties wounded O.R. 2.	
	28.10.17		Trench routine. Batt" were relieved by the 2/8.13th WORCESTERS in the front & support trenches. Casualties NIL	
	29.10.17		Trench routine. Working parties. Lt Col. BALFOUR D.S.O. (Glos Regt.) took over command of the Batt". Casualties NIL	
	30.10.17		Trench Routine. Working Parties. Casualties NIL	
	31.10.17		Trench Routine. Working Parties. Casualties killed O.R. 1	

A. V. Rose Troop
2/7 th Worcestershire Regt

183
217th Bn. Worcestershire Regt. 1st
9/5/19

War Diary.

Army Form C. 2118.

WAR DIARY
of
INTELLIGENCE SUMMARY.

(Erase heading not required.) 2/7th Bn. The WORCESTERSHIRE REGT.

Title pages Sheet No. I

Instructions regarding War Diaries and Intelligence Summaries are contained in F.S. Regs., Part II. and the Staff Manual respectively. Title pages will be prepared in manuscript.

Place	Date	Hour	Summary of Events and Information	Remarks and references to Appendices
FAMPOUX	1-11-17		Bn in support. CHEMICAL WORKS sector. Working parties, Casualties Nil	GAS
"	2-11-17		Working parties. 2/Lieut BRIDGE G.F.R, 2/Lieut ELFORD & 2/Lieut GRIFFITHS B.L. reported for duty from 7th Worcn Bott. Woxon Regt. No 203016 Pte JONES F.R. presented with Parchment for gallantry by G.O.C. Div. No 201978 L/C Bridge W.J. and No 203838 Pte Drake T.H. awarded military medals. Casualties Nil.	h.T.B3
"	3-11-17		Trench routine. Relieved 2/8 Bott Worc Regt in front line. Chemical Works sector. 2/Lieut Sub-Lieton 2/Lieut Jadden C.M. proceeded to H Q. of C. + Coy. Casualties Nil.	h.T.B3
CHEMICAL WORKS	4-11-17		Trench routine. No 203016 Pte JONES F.R. awarded military medal. Casualties Nil	h.T.B3
"	5-11-17		Trench routine. Night of 4/5 & 5/6 2/Lt WILLMORE J. MISSING, of a patrol.	h & G3
"	6-11-17		2 O.Rs. Wounded. O.R. 1.	h.& G3
"	7-11-17		Trench routine. Casualties Nil	h.& G3
"			Trench routine. CAPT GOODWIN H awarded MILITARY CROSS. No. 201174 Sergt JOLLEY B awarded D.C.M. Armed body of Germans endeavoured to enter one of our Saps but were driven off leaving 2 wounded.	
"	8-11-17		Casualties 1 O.R. KILLED	h.T.B3
"	9-11-17		Trench routine. Casualties missing 6 R1 (patrol) Wounded 7 O.R. Billetted in the PRISON ARRAS. Bott relieved at night by 7/8 Batt O.B.L.I. (184 Bde).	h.T.B3
ARRAS	10-11-17		Interior economy, bathing and general cleaning up. Casualties Nil	h.T.B3

Army Form C. 2118.

WAR DIARY
INTELLIGENCE SUMMARY

(Erase heading not required.) 2/7: Bat: Worcestershire Regt.

SHEET No 2

Instructions regarding War Diaries and Intelligence Summaries are contained in F.S. Regs., Part II. and the Staff Manual respectively. Title pages will be prepared in manuscript.

Place	Date	Hour	Summary of Events and Information	Remarks and references to Appendices
ARRAS	11-11-17		Church Parade. 2/Lieut WARD P.F.S. reported for duty from 7th Reserve Bat WORCS. REGT. Reinforcements O.R. 85 joined. Casualties Nil.	A. & B.
"	12-11-17		Working parties. Casualties Nil.	A. & B.
"	13-11-17		Working parties. Casualties Nil. No 201047 Sergt KENDALL J. awarded M.M.	A. & B.
"	14-11-17		" Casualties Nil.	A. & B.
"	15-11-17		" "	A. & B.
"	16-11-17		Training. C.O's inspection. Casualties Nil.	A. & B.
"	17-11-17		Brigade Ministry Meeting. Working parties Casualties Nil.	A. & B.
"	18-11-17		Church Parade. Working parties. Casualties Nil.	A. & B.
"	19-11-17		Bathing. Working parties. Football match. Bn Boxing competition	A. & B.
"	20-11-17		Casualties Nil.	A. & B.
"	20-11-17		Training. Working parties. Casualties Nil.	A. & B.
"	21-11-17		Relieved 4th Batt. R. WARWICKSHIRE REGT in GREENLAND HILL Right Sub Sector. Relief complete without incident 5.30 P.M. Casualties Nil.	A. & B.
GREENLAND HILL.	22-11-17		Bn. Routine. Working Parties. 2/Lt HANGAR A.C. rejoined Batt. Casualties Nil.	A. & B.
"	23-11-17		"	A. & B.
"	24-11-17		"	A. & B.
"	25-11-17		"	A. & B.
"	26-11-17		" No 203534 Sergt Johnson W. awarded MILITARY MEDAL	A. & B.

Army Form C. 2118.

WAR DIARY
INTELLIGENCE SUMMARY.

(Erase heading not required.) 2/7th BATT. WORCESTERSHIRE REGT.

SHEET No 3

Place	Date	Hour	Summary of Events and Information	Remarks and references to Appendices
GREEN LAND HILL	27/11/17		General routine. Working Parties. Casualties Nil.	Ah 103.
ARRAS	28/11/17		General routine. Batt. relieved by 6/7th R.S.F's and 11th ARGYLES (15th Div) completely without incident. 1 Lieut BOSWELL.H.E. & SYKES J.S. reported for duty, also reinforcements 2 O.R. Lt DRAKE rejoined from NZ Gun Cy. Casualties Nil.	Ah 10.
"	29/11/17		Bathing. Cleaning up. Billets shelled by 8" gun. Casualties 2 O.R. KILLED: 3 O.R. WOUNDED. (B Coy.)	Ah 103.
"	30/11/17		Bathing. Inspection of Coys by C.O. Batt entrained at DAINVILLE and detrained at BAPAUME, marching by Brig Gen'l Billets at TRESCAULT. Snowshot however by road stating 7.0 AM. Casualties Nil.	Got Ah 63.

C.A.Thompson
Capt & A.G.
Lt 2/7th WORCESTERSHIRE REGT.

December 1917

War Diary
of
2/7th Bn. The Worcestershire Regt.

Army Form C. 2118.

WAR DIARY
of
INTELLIGENCE SUMMARY.

(Erase heading not required.) THE 2/7 BN THE WORCESTERSHIRE REGT (T.F)

Instructions regarding War Diaries and Intelligence Summaries are contained in F.S. Regs., Part II. and the Staff Manual respectively. Title pages will be prepared in manuscript.

Place	Date	Hour	Summary of Events and Information	Remarks and references to Appendices
TRESCAULT	1.12.17		Relieved a Batt of the K.R.R.C. at LA VACQUERIE nick - relief completed 1.0.0 m night of the 1/2nd. Casualties - Wounded. O.R. 2. Trench Routine. Casualties - Wounded. O.R. 4.	
LA VACQUERIE SECTOR	2.12.17			
"	3.12.17		Batt: stood to all day - attacks on B. 572 were withdrawn from front to front line. Transport & P.M. this moved from ROYAULCOURT to EQUANCOURT. Casualties. 2/7 SYKES. W.5 having believed killed - KILLED O.R. 6 - Wounded CAPT MANUEL R.A.M.C (att 2) and O.R. 12 (inclg 1 at duty) Lieut Rastrick LT ERICKSON, B.J. (US Army R.C.) took up duties as Medical Officer. Casualties - killed. O.R. 2. Wounded 2/LT BOSWELL H.E. — LT FLINT, T.F. (to) arang. O.R. 10	
"	4.12.17			
"	5.12.17		Trench Routine - Relieved on the evening by the 2/1 BUCKS BN (184 Bde) & moved to support line East of HAVRINCOURT WOOD. Casualties - nil.	
"	6.12.17		Eight shelters & dugouts. Casualties. Wounded - CAPT GOODWIN, H.	
"	7.12.17		Working parties on trenches & roads. Casualties - Wounded O.R. 1 (Accidental)	
"	8.12.17		Working parties on trenches & roads. 2/LT BOSWELL H.B. transferred to ENGLAND (wounded) Casualties - Nil.	
"	9.12.17		Working parties on trenches & roads. Casualties - Nil	
"	9.12.17		Relieved the 2/4 OXFORDS (184 Bde) in LA VACQUERIE SECTOR (Rt front). Relief complete 4.0 p.m. Reinforcements from 61st Div Depot. O.R. 1. Casualties. Wounded O.R. 2. Trench Routine. Casualties O.R. 1 (accidental)	
"	10.12.17		Trench Routine - Heavy hostile shelling of MILLERS PLOUGH & BEAUCHAMP RIDGE. CAPT GOODWIN H. transferred to ENGLAND wounded. Casualties - killed. LT COL BALFOUR R.P. C.O. & Ots R2. Wounded whilst examining gun ore) Wounded O.R. 1 (Accidental)	
"	11.12.17			
"	12.12.17			

Army Form C. 2118.

WAR DIARY
of
INTELLIGENCE SUMMARY.

(Erase heading not required.) THE 2/7 BN THE WORCESTERSHIRE REGT (T.F.)

Instructions regarding War Diaries and Intelligence Summaries are contained in F. S. Regs., Part II. and the Staff Manual respectively. Title pages will be prepared in manuscript.

Place	Date	Hour	Summary of Events and Information	Remarks and references to Appendices
LA MACQUERIE SECTOR	13.12.17		Lines Routine. 3 of the enemy exploded near bombing store at R.21.C.2.7. belonging to 18.5 Div. 161. I.R. 2nd Bde. 8th Coy. MAJOR LAWSON. M.D. (11th Hussars) assumed command of Batt. Casualties - Wounded O.R. 2	
"	14.12.17		Lines Routine. Relieved in the evening by the 2/8 Bn WORCS moved into Reserve Line at VILLERS PLOUICH. Casualties. Wounded O.R. 2	
VILLERS PLOUICH	15.12.17		Working & carrying parties - Salvage work. Casualties - NIL	
"	16.12.17		Salvage work. Relieved in the evening by the 2/1 st BUCKS (184 Bde) & moved to HAVRINCOURT WOOD. Reinforcements O.R. 3 (Signallers) from 174 Inf. f. Bse. Casualties - NIL	
HAVRINCOURT WOOD	17.12.17		Working & carrying parties. CAPT BLACKBORNE; G.M.I. admitted Hospital (Sick) Casualties - NIL	
"	18.12.17		Working & carrying parties - Casualties - NIL	
"	19.12.17		Working & carrying parties - Casualties - NIL	
"	20.12.17		Relieved 2/1st Bucks at VILLERS PLOUICH (support line) at 6.0 p.m. 2/LT GRAZEBROOK C.J. rejoined (n duty. CAPT MANUEL J. RAM.C. (attd) reported from Hospital. AWARDS - MILITARY CROSS - CAPT MANUEL J. R.A.M.C. (attd.) Casualties - NIL	
VILLERS PLOUICH	21.12.17		Working Parties - Salvage Parties. Casualties - NIL	
"	22.12.17		Relieved by HOWE BN. R.N.D. at 5.35 p.m. moved to HAVRINCOURT WOOD. Casualties - NIL	
HAVRINCOURT WOOD	23.12.17	11.0 a.m.	18th Left HAVRINCOURT WOOD & marched to Camp at ETRICOURT. Casualties - NIL	
ETRICOURT	24.12.17		Transport left EQUANCOURT (nr MORCOURT) (Somme) arriving at 9 p.m. 18th left ETRICOURT by train at 12.0 noon, detrained at PLATEAU STN. TROOPS marched to Billets at MORCOURT arriving at 5.0 p.m. Casualties - NIL	

Army Form C. 2113.

WAR DIARY
or
INTELLIGENCE SUMMARY.

(Erase heading not required.) THE 2/4 B⁵ THE WORCESTERSHIRE REG⁵ (T.F.)

Instructions regarding War Diaries and Intelligence Summaries are contained in F. S. Regs., Part II. and the Staff Manual respectively. Title pages will be prepared in manuscript.

Place	Date	Hour	Summary of Events and Information	Remarks and references to Appendices
MORCOURT	25/12/17		18⁵ & Company training. Casualties. NIL	
"	26.12.17		" " " "	
"	27.12.17		" " " "	
"	28.12.17		18⁵ Company training. 2/Lt DUDLEY. A.M. FOX.J.N. & CULLIS C.J reported from Reinforcements O.R 2. Casualties reported O.R. 5. Casualties NIL	
"	29.12.17		18⁵ Xmas Dinner - Casualties NIL ?	
"	30.12.17		Church Parade, Casualties NIL	
"	31.12.17	8.30 a.m	18⁵ marched & were billeted at MARCELCAVE arriving at 11.14 am Casualties NIL	

R.F. Rowe Major
fr O.C. 2/4/13 Worcester Reg⁵

CONFIDENTIAL.

XVII Corps No.G.5/29

61st Division

The following are the remarks made by the Army Commander on the raid carried out by the 2/7th Worcestershire Regt. and 2/4th Gloucestershire Regt. on the enemy's front in Squares I.14.a. and I.8.c. on 24th October:

"Nothing could have been better than the spirit displayed".

(Sd) V.JOHNSON, Major,
for Brigadier-General,
General Staff.

H.Q. XVII Corps.
1st November 1917.

TO:
4 Glosters   8 Worcesters
6 Glosters   183 M.G.Coy.
7 Worcesters 183 T.M.B.

For your information.

BHQ
3.11.17.

Capt.,
A/Bde.Major, 183 Inf.Bde.

RAID CARRIED OUT BY THE 2/7th. BATTALION
THE WORCESTERSHIRE REGIMENT.

Refs. FAMPOUX TRENCH MAP.

OFFICERS: Capt. H. GOODWIN, O.C. Raiding Party.
            2nd. Lieut. H.V.G. ROBINSON.

On the 24th. inst. a party of 2 Officers and 50 O.R. were detailed to raid the enemy's front line and support trenches South of the Railway cutting, with the object of:-

(a.) Destroying dug-outs.
(b.) Inflicting casualties on the enemy.
(c.) Obtaining identifications.

The points of entry are marked "A", and "B" on sketch.

There was a previous intense bombardment by the Corps Heavy Artillery, 61st. Divisional Artillery, and 15th. Divisional Artillery from zero to zero plus 20.

At zero (2.30.p.m.) smoke was put out on the Southern flank of the assault; smoke was again put out at zero plus 80 and the smoke barrage was kept up until zero plus 100.

The Raiding party was to go no further north than the Railway cutting and no further South than the trench junction I.14.c. 19.20. marked Q. on the sketch.

No documents, letters, papers, orders or any articles by which the enemy might get an identification were carried by any of the raiders.

The dress for the Raiders was; stripped belt, rifle and bayonet, steel helmet, and box respirator in the alert position: magazines were fully charged and ten rounds of S.A.A. were carried in each trouser pocket.

The Intelligence man in each section carried a sharp pocket knife and two sand-bags.

Each section carried; 4 P. bombs, 16 Mills grenades, and 2 battle wire cutters.

The return signal was - G.'s sounded on the bugle and Red Very Lights fired from our parapet.

At zero minus 10 all were assembled in the deep dug-outs in Cocoa Alley where they stopped during the bombardment. At zero plus 50 the Raiders moved up Cocoa Alley to their jumping off places which were in the advanced front line of the Left Company. There the scaling ladders were fixed opposite the gaps in our own wire.

At zero plus 80 (3.50.p.m.) the bombardment of the enemy trenches having re-commenced the leading parties climbed the ladders, and advanced to the assault. They at once came under a heavy Hostile Artillery and Machine Gun barrage which made it extremely difficult for the columns to form up as arranged beforehand under the protection of our own barrage.

At zero plus 84 the parties advanced on the enemy's line. During the whole of the advance across " No Man's Land" to the German lines the enemy (who was in considerable force in his front line) stood up and opened fire with rifles and Machine Guns, Machine Gun fire coming chiefly from the strong point on the right and a Machine Gun in the centre of the position which was being attacked. In spite of this the party reached the enemy wire. At this juncture a large number of hand-grenades and stick bombs were thrown at them, the rifle and machine gun fire of the enemy still being intense.

During the advance a Lewis Gunner spotted one of the machine guns and opened fire on it immediately and endeavoured to stop it firing. To avoid delay he fired the lewis gun from his shoulder in a standing position.

Sheet 2.

When the remainder of the Men came up to those near the wire, covering fire was opened and the first parties started to go through the wire. Immediately, the Germans started running back over the top and down the trench towards the Railway cutting. Only a few of them succeeded in getting away alive so accurate was the fire of our Men.
A German Officer jumped on his parapet and attempted to rally his Men but was immediately shot by one of the leading raiders.
Covering fire was kept up on the flanks of the Men getting through the wire, which they succeeded in doing. All the time some of the enemy were running across the top; none of these were seen to get away.
By this time some of the Men had got through the wire. A Lance Corporal spotted a hostile Machine Gunner firing his gun; he attacked him, shot him dead and smashed up the gun. The parties in the trench proceeded along it bombing the dug-outs, the Intelligence men obtaining identifications.

The trench was deserted except that about 30 dead bodies of the enemy, of whom most had been accounted for by our rifle fire, were found there.
The enemy trench was in good condition, apparently having been little damaged by shell fire: it was not revetted and no duck-boards were laid, but fire steps, cubby holes and small dug-outs were found to be in good condition. The size of the small dug-outs was about 10 feet by 6 feet.

At this point it was found to be impossible owing to the strength of the enemy wire to get sufficient men together in time to cut off the retreating enemy.
The retreating Germans had reached their close support line about 70 yards away, and were bringing heavy machine gun and rifle fire to bear on the remainder of the men who were crawling through the wire. Those in the trench were being bombed.
At zero plus 95 the object of the raid having been accomplished, the O.C. Raid decided to withdraw and sent back a Runner with a message to have the bugle sounded and the Red Very lights fired.
The party came back in small groups as far as the middle of " No Man's Land " where they opened rapid fire on the enemy who was now manning his trenches strongly.
The last unwounded man of the Raiding Party reached our lines at 4.27.p.m.
Organised parties were immediately sent out to bring in the wounded.
During the whole of the hostile bombardment no single casualty occurred among the men who were holding our own line.

Major,

Commanding, 2/7th. Battalion The Worcestershire Regiment.

25.10.17.

SECRET.   (Copy).   G.C. 40/11/d.

XVII Corps.
----

1. I beg to forward report by G.O.C., 183rd. Inf. Bde. on the daylight raid carried out on the 24th. October 1917, by the 2/4th. Gloucester Regt. and 2/7th. Worcestershire Regt,. of the Brigade under his Command.

2. The use of the rifle and Lewis Gun throughout the operation illustrates that the correct application of fire by infantry is still sufficient to cover their movements against an entrenched enemy.

3. I consider that the success of the raid was due to the resources and leadership of the commanders and the dash and steadiness of the men.

4. Great credit is due to Brig-Gen. A.H. SPOONER, D.S.O., Commanding 183rd. Inf. Bde., Lieut-Col. D.C. BARNSLEY, Comdg. 2/4th. Glosters, and Major A.V. ROWE Commanding 2/7th. Worcesters, for organising the operations at short notice.

5. I shall be bringing to your notice the names of some of the officers, N.C.O's and men of the raiding parties in a separate recommendation.

6. The Artillery was not so well registered on these trenches (time for registration being short and observation difficult) as has proved to be the case in previous Divisional operations on this front.

25 October. 1917.   )Sgd). Colin Mackenzie.
                                                  Major General.
                                           Comdg. 61st. Division.

61st. Division.

Reports from the two units engaged in the afternoon of the 24th. are forwarded herewith. The smoke screens put up on either flank of the attack were apparently most successful in preventing M.G. fire from the flanks, th M.G. fire mentioned in the reports being from the part of the line assaulted, and it does not appear to have been at all heavy. The gap in the wire on the north of the Railway Cutting was apparently very narrow, and covered by a Machine Gun; Lieut. SHIPWAY therefore deployed his men in shell holes immediately in front of the wire, and opened fire, accounting for 8 Germans who were manning their parapets. A light Machine Gun was observed coming up from the North, and as it got into position the two men firing it were shot, and the gun fell back into the trench. It was put back on the parapet later, and fired from the bottom of the trench, the bullets going several feet over the heads of our men. All the Germans that could be seen were shot, but seeing the party on the South of the Railway Cutting were withdrawing, Lieut. SHIPWAY gave the order to return.   This was done successfully without casualties.

On the South the advance seems to have been most ably carried out, the men covering each other's advance through the gap with rifle fire, and then fighting their way up the trenches. The men's blood was up, no prisoners were taken, but identifications were taken by men specially detailed for the purpose.

Unfortunately, the barrage on the enemy's front line seems to have been over the trenches in each case, thus enabling the Germans to man their parapet. The attack was most gallantly pushed, and all leaders were more than satisfied with their afternoon's work.

The hostile artillery was fairly heavy on our trenches, and a few of the casualties were caused in getting back to deep dug-outs in our line.

On the lowest estimate 30 Germans were killed on the South, and a Machine Gun destroyed; 20 - 30 Germans on the North.

Our casualties were, under the circumstances, very light:-

    2/4th. GLOSTERS. - 2 Killed.   4 wounded.

    2/7th. Worcesters- 1 Officer) killed.
                        4 O.R.   )

                       10. wounded.
                       2. missing.

Considering the two Infantry units had only 36 hour's notice of the operation, I consider it was greatly to the credit of all concerned that it was so successfully carried out. Both parties had taped out the enemy's trenches, and gone through the drill on the morning of the raid.

                                                      (Sgd). A.H. Spooner.
                                                                Brig-Genl.
25.10.17.   Commanding 183rd. Ingantry Brigade.

RIGHT ATTACK.

Our guns opened at 2.30.p.m. for the preliminary bombardment until 2.50.p.m.

During the pause of one hour "C" Coy. 2/7th. Worcester Regt. the Right raiding party, reached their jumping-off point, and were in position by 3.45.p.m.

Punctually at 3.50.p.m. our barrage came down on the enemy trenches, but again little fell on his front line. Our shrapnel bursts were high.

The attacking party left our trenches as the artillery opened and immediately came under Machine Gun fire.

They advanced across NO MAN'S LAND by means of rushes from shell-hole to shell-hole, to avoid casualties. In spite of these precautions 3 casualties were caused on the way over. 2nd. Lieut. ROBINSON was leading the most forward party, Capt. GOODWIN directed operations from the centre.

When the first wave got within 30 yards of the German wire they were met by a shower of bombs. This hung up the party for one or two minutes. The rear parties came up and the party succeeded in jumping into the enemy's line. They first encountered a Machine Gun detachment and bayoneted them all; the gun was in a fixed position and could not be brought away so it was destroyed. Proceeding further up the enemy's trenches another party of 10 men were encountered, these showed fight and so were all killed with the bayonet.

Germans could be seen running to the rear over the top, and our men immediately opened fire and claim several hits.

Shortly after, Capt. GOODWIN signalled the recall signal and the party returned to our lines in twos and threes.

It is estimated that about 30 of the enemy were killed, and one Machine Gun damaged.

The raiders report that the enemy's wire was badly damaged but there was no clear gap.

Owing to the heavy hostile retaliation the raiders were ordered into deep dug-outs with the exception of a few N.C.O's and men who remained to get in the wounded. Of these, Coy. S.M. SIMKINS, Sergt. SALT and Corpl. BRIDGES rendered the greatest possible service, Sergt. SALT twice going out under Machine Gun fire, Corpl. BRIDGES was unfortunately wounded whilst doing a similar thing.

Estimated casualties:-

1 Officer, 2nd. Lt. ROBINSON. missing (believed killed)

2 men - missing.
4 men - killed.
10 men - wounded.

Shoulder straps were collected by the Intelligence men and brought back.

Corps

S E C R E T - NOT TO BE TAKEN BEYOND BATTALION H.Q. IN THE LINE.
61st DIVISION INTELLIGENCE SUMMARY No. 31.
From 12 noon 24th to 12 noon 25th Octr.

1. OPERATIONS. "A" - OUR OWN.

An intense bombardment by Divisional and Corps artillery was carried out yesterday afternoon between 2.30 p.m. and 2.50 p.m., and at the same time smoke was discharged on the flanks of the areas bombarded. At 3.50 p.m. a barrage was put down on the enemy's front line, again accompanied by smoke on flanks, and two parties, each of about 50 men, left our lines to raid the enemy's trenches immediately N. and S. of the railway. The southern party, composed of men of the WORCESTER Regt., came under M.G. fire when advancing across NO MAN'S LAND, but when our barrage lifted succeeded in getting through the wire and entering the enemy's trench. Here a number of Germans were found; one M.G. team of six, who attempted to escape down the trench, were all bayoneted and their M.G. destroyed, as it was fixed to the parapet. Several other Germans were killed in the trench, and rifle fire was successfully brought to bear on men who attempted to run back over the top. Shoulder-straps were obtained from dead Germans, showing them to belong to 457 I.R. (normal). No prisoners were taken, but at least 30 casualties were inflicted on the enemy.

The left party, men of the GLOUCESTER Regt., also came under M.G. fire when crossing NO MAN'S LAND, and were unable to find a gap in the wire. Meanwhile the enemy manned his parapet and opened rifle fire, to which our men vigorously replied with bombs and rifle fire. During the course of this fire fight a M.G. crew firing from I.14.a. 95.95 were knocked out, and several of the enemy who showed themselves over the parapet were killed. It is estimated that about 10 or 15 Germans were accounted for. The party then withdrew.

Our casualties in this operation were light.

At 9.30 p.m. last night a party of the ROYAL BERKSHIRE REGIMENT, commanded by Captain J.A. REEVES, after an intense 3 minutes bombardment, entered the enemy's front line at I.2.c.1.7, and cleared it for 100 yards on either side. Nine Germans were killed, seven dugouts bombed, and a M.G. captured. As a result of the preliminary bombardment a number of dead were found in the enemy's front line, and it is possible that the enemy had been caught assembling for a small raid on our trenches.

A prisoner captured on the night 23rd/24th further south had indicated the possibility of a raid in this neighbourhood.

Identifications of the 459 I.R. were obtained.
Our casualties were 4 wounded.

- - - - - - - - - - - - - - - - - -

Artillery.
At 2.30 p.m. our 18-pdrs. and 4.5" hows. bombarded the enemy's trenches in I.8.d. and I.14.b, in cooperation with the area bombardment carried out by the Heavy Artillery. The 18-pdr. batteries fired smoke shell and placed a screen on the flanks of the area bombarded from I.8.c.8.7 to I.9.c.1.4 along WALNUT Trench and I.14.b.5.9 to I.9.c.2.2 along the RAILWAY CUTTING.

At 3.50 p.m. the enemy's trenches in I.8.a, b, and c. were bombarded according to programme in support of the daylight raid.

At 9.30 p.m. the enemy's trenches in I.1.b. and I.2.a, c, and d. were bombarded in support of the night raid.

Harassing fire was kept up in bursts from 7.30 to 9 p.m. in the hope of catching the enemy relief forecasted by deserter from I.R.457.

Trench Mortars & Machine Guns.
Our T.M. and M.G. acted in cooperation with the artillery in connection with the raiding operations. M.Gs. were also very active with harassing fire directed against the suspected enemy relief.

(P.T.O.).

(2)

Aerial.
Our aeroplanes were very active in connection with the afternoon operations.

"B" - THE ENEMY'S.

Artillery.
In reply to the bombardment at 2.30 p.m. the enemy replied with 4.2" on Station, Railway Cutting and Chemical Works in I.13.
At 3.15 p.m., on conclusion of our bombardment, the enemy put down a 4.2" barrage on our front line and COSTA ALLEY to the Railway.
At 3.20 p.m. his fire increased, rounds of 77mm and 4.2" falling in H.17.d, H.17.b, and H.18.a. After our raid at 3.50 p.m. shelling on these points was renewed, and FAMPOUX was shelled with 4.2"
After the night raid hostile artillery activity was less pronounced. Practically the same targets as before were engaged, but his fire was weak in comparison. A few 77mm fell around our battery position in H.14.c, and some 4.2" on OAK and CURSE.

Machine Guns.
Enemy M.G. showed considerable activity during the operations, and fired bursts over our lines throughout the night.

Aerial.
Hostile 'planes patrolled our lines at low altitude during the afternoon raid.

2. INTELLIGENCE.

Identifications. I.R.459, I.R.457 - 236th Divn. NORMAL.
In the course of the raid carried out at 3.50 p.m., 24th Octr., identification was obtained of the 11th Coy. III/I.R. (This confirms the statement of deserter captured before the raid).
A shoulder-strap was obtained bearing the number "135", a regiment from which the 457 I.R. had received a draft.
In the night raid the 459 I.R. was identified.

Movement.
Considerable activity was observed near the Cemetery in FRESNES.
A party of 40 men and several transport wagons observed on the road from BIACHE to the STATION.

Information from Patrols.
The gap in enemy wire at I.3.a.4.0 is still open and has not been worked on.
The enemy was not occupying any advanced posts in this vicinity.

General.
At 6.30 a.m. columns of smoke were seen rising from buildings in VITRY.
An explosion occurred in HAMBLAIN-LES-PRES at 9.35 a.m., and clouds of smoke went up.

Light Signals.
During the two raids the enemy used a great variety of light signals.
It would appear that for the moment his S.O.S. is red lights or golden rain, and that green lights signify "No attack on this front".

for G.S., 61 Divn.

ANNEXE TO 61st DIV. SUMMARY No.31 - 25.10.17.

Preliminary examination of Deserter from 10/III/I.R.457,
who entered our lines in I.14.a. (north of Rly.) 24.10.17.

Method of escape.

Prisoner, who was in the line for the first time, left his front line with the connivance of a friendly sentry, and gave himself up to one of our sentries.
He did not know that our attack was imminent.

History.

Prisoner was of the 1918 Class, and was called up at the October "Muster" 1916. He was allowed to remain at work in a large newly finished munition works at OBERHAUSEN, where he was employed. On Augt. 15th 1917 he was "reklamirt" (combed out), and sent for training to the I.R.605 at CREFELD. Here he received only six weeks' training, and at the end of September came to the Feldrekruten Depot at ABSCON. Four days later he was drafted with 700 others to the 236 Div. in its present sector. Prisoner's Coy. received a draft of about 15 men.

Method of holding line.

All four Coys. are in the front line. One Coy. (11) is south of Railway, and 3 Coys. north, in the following order N. to S - 12, 10, 9. The line is very lightly held, and prisoner states that he was enabled to escape by the fact that there were only 3 sentries on his Coy. front during the day.
By night the Coy. front is held by 3 double sentries, 4 M.G. with 2 men to each, and double sentries in each of the three saps.
Coy. trench strength is about 70.

Relief.

The next relief was due night 24th/25th October, the I Battn. in BREBIERES relieving the III Battn. then holding the line. Route of relief is as follows :- from BREBIERES - along south side of canal to BIACHE, where canal is crossed; thence to BIACHE STN., along the Railway cutting to WHALE Trench, and along WINE to front line

Trench Mortars.

Prisoner having been only six days in the line knows little of T.M., but had seen 3 granatenwerfer in the support line.

State of trenches.

The general state of the trenches is bad. There is practically no revetting, and only a few duckboards in the C.Ts. Considerable work is being done on improvements to trenches, with a view to laying more boards.

H.Q. and Trench Names.

Coy. H.Q. are at about I.8.d.25.25. The trench in which these H.Q. are situated is known as LOCKSTADTER GRABEN throughout its length to its junction with WHALE.
Battn. H.Q. The H.Q. of the Battn. in line are situated in the Railway Cutting about 300 yds. East of the junction with WHALE.
The H.Q. of the Support Battn. are a little further back between the Railway Cutting and BIACHE.
Prisoner is positive on this point, as he has a friend who is an orderly at Battn. H.Q.
WHALE Trench, north of the Railway in I.10.a, is known as MUHLEN GRABEN.

Casualties.

On the night 22nd/23rd the 10th Coy. had 2 men of their own patrol wounded by the sentries in one of the saps, who challenged and got no answer.
The same night the 9th Coy. had 6 casualties from our artillery fire.

(P.T.O.).

I.R.605 Prisoner joined I.R.605 on 17th Augt. in CREFELD. On
I.R.614. 3rd Septr. the regiment moved to OLFEN (III Bn.),
LUDWIGHAUSEN (II Bn.), and DULMEN (I Bn.).

On Septr. 27th practically the whole of the I.R.605 entrained at SELM, where they were joined by a draft from the 614 I.R, which was guarding the German - Dutch frontier. The whole contingent was conveyed to the Feldrekruten Depot at ABSCOW.

Moral. Moral would appear to be very low. Prisoner did not make any particular secret of his intention to desert, and had tried to persuade a friend to accompany him; the latter being due for leave in a few days decided to postpone the event.

FRENCH WIRELESS.
PARIS. 3 p.m. 24.10.17.

German prisoners now number 8,000, including 160 officers, of whom three are colonels in command of regiments.

Prisoners belong to 8 different divisions, of which two are Guards.

The three colonels confirm the fact that 2 German Divisions in reserve behind the front were engaged on 23rd, and suffered heavily.

11.45 p.m.

Prisoners are over 8,000, and other booty includes :-
  70 guns,
  30 Minenwerfer.
  80 Machine guns.

Captain Goodwin's Report.
-----oOo------

At Zero minus 10 we all assembled in the deep dugout in COC trench where we stoped/during the bombardment till Zero plus 60. At Zero plus 60 we moved out and proceeded to our kicking off places which were in the advanced front line of the left Company. At Zero plus 70 we fixed the ladders at two places opposite the gaps in our wire. At Zero plus 80 the bombardment recommenced and our leading parties climbed the ladders and rushed to the assault; they were at once met with a heavy machine gun barrage which made it impossible to form up in our own barrage in columns as arranged beforehand. When everybody was over the top we rushed forward in one wave. The whole time going across to the German lines the enemy(who was in considerable force, in his front trench) stood up and sniped at us with rifles, machine gun fire continuing the whole time from the strong point on our right. As we neared the German wire our leading men (strength about 20 rifles) opened rapid fire at the Germans in the front line from the outer edge of the German wire and the Germans threw great numbers of stick bombs and hand grenades at them, as many as 10 being counted in the air at the same time. Then also our Lewis Gunner fired the Lewis Gun from his shoulder, trying to stop the machine gun fire from the right. Immediately the Germans started some running back over the top and some running down the trench towards the Railway Cutting. A German Officer jumped up and attempted to rally his men but was immediately shot by one of our leading men. The party of about 8 of our men then proceeded to work their way through the wire, which was thick. During the time this party was working through the wire the parties on their flanks opened covering fire with their rifles on the Germans running across the top. By this time those men who had crawled through the wire jumped into the trench, A Corporal shooting a machine gunner and smashing the machine gun. They then proceeded along the trench(and found it deserted) firing on the Germans retreating down the trench. At this point it was found

(Continued)

impossible to get sufficient men in together and quickly enough to be able to cut off the retreating enemy. We then proceeded to collect identifications off the dead Germans, mostly accounted for by our rifle fire. By this time the Germans had reached their close support line 70 yards away, and were bringing heavy fire both from rifles and machine guns to bear on the rest of our men who were preparing to crawl through the wire.

At Zero plus 95, the object of the raid having been accomplished, under these circumstances the O.C. raid decided to withdraw. We came back in groups of twos and threes and collected together in the middle of NO MANS LAND where we halted, turned round and opened rapid fire for a few seconds on the Germans close support line which by this time was fully manned by the enemy.

Capt Goodwin's Raid.

January 1918

War Diary
~ of ~
2/7th Batt. The Worcestershire Regt.

Army Form C. 2118.

WAR DIARY
or
INTELLIGENCE SUMMARY.
(Erase heading not required.)

Army Form: 2/7 a Batt WORCESTERSHIRE REGT

SHEET No. 1

Place	Date	Hour	Summary of Events and Information	Remarks and references to Appendices
MARCELCAVE	1918 Jan 1st		Company training and specialist training. Capt Engwood M.S. 200/09. R.Q.M.S. Humphreys L.W. 201304 2/Lt Eidaway W.H. specially mentioned in Dispatches. Authority Supplement London Gazette 18-12-17. Casualties Nil.	A 20
"	Jan 2nd		Company training and specialist training. Casualties Nil.	A 20
"	Jan 3		Company training and specialist training. Casualties Nil.	A 20
"	Jan 4		Company training and specialist training. Firing on range. 2/Lt PEARCE E.S. reported for duty from 4th Gar. Bn. Worc Regt. Reinforcements O.R. 17 (1 from 2/8 Bn Worc Regt.) Casualties Nil.	A 20
"	Jan 5		Company and specialist training. Firing on range. Casualties Nil.	A 20
"	Jan 6		Church parade. 2/Lt THINTON E. reported for duty from 4th Res Bn Worc Regt. 2/Lt SHERLOCK T.P. admitted to hospital sick. Casualties Nil.	A 20
"	Jan 7		Battalion left MARCELCAVE 8.0 am. Marched to ROYE (16 miles) and billeted. Arrived 4.0 pm. Casualties Nil.	A 20
ROYE.	Jan 8		Interior economy. "B" Coy - representing 183 Brigade - inspected on ROYE SQUARE by General Sir H. de la P. GOUGH K.C.B., K.C.V.O. Commanding 5th Army. Casualties Nil.	A 20

WAR DIARY or INTELLIGENCE SUMMARY

Army Form C. 2118.

2/7th Batt WORCESTERSHIRE REGT SHEET No II

Place	Date	Hour	Summary of Events and Information	Remarks and references to Appendices
ROYE	1918. Jan. 9		Battalion left ROYE at 10.0 a.m. Bn H.Q. "C" + "D" Companies marched to BUNY (9 miles). "A" + "B" Companies marched to CROIX MOLIGNEAUX (7 miles) Capt (acting Major) BOUCHER M.C. ordered to ENGLAND for duty with Bank Corps and started off this afternoon. Casualties nil.	16-10
BUNY and CROIX MOLIGNEAUX	Jan. 10		"C" and "D" Companies engaged in wiring trenches "A" + "B" Coys - Company training. Reinforcements O.R. 27 (1 from 10 Batt Worc Regt). Casualties Nil.	6-13
"	Jan 11		Company and specialist training. Lt SMITH. M.S. (14th Worcesters) 2/Lt HASSALL. C. (5th Worcs) 2/Lt FINCH L.T. (5th Worcs) Reported for duty. 2/Lt LAMBETH. (5th Worcs) 2/Lt THOMAS (5th Worcs) Casualties Nil.	
"	12th		Company training. 2/Lt TWIST. W.M. Commenced duties as sub-area Commandant "B" Area. Casualties Nil.	6-15
"	13th		Company and specialist training. Casualties Nil.	6-16
"	14th		Company and specialist training. Major ROWE A. F. assumed command of Battalion during temporary absence of Lt. Col. LAMBURN. Casualties Nil.	10-14

Army Form C. 2118.

WAR DIARY
or
INTELLIGENCE SUMMARY.
(Erase heading not required.)

SHEET No III 2/1⁴ᵗʰ Batt WORCESTERSHIRE

Instructions regarding War Diaries and Intelligence Summaries are contained in F. S. Regs., Part II. and the Staff Manual respectively. Title pages will be prepared in manuscript.

Place	Date	Hour	Summary of Events and Information	Remarks and references to Appendices
BUNY and CROIX MOLIGNEAUX	9ᵗʰ Jan 16	10:00am	Bn H.Q., "C" & "D" left BUNY and marched to GERMAINE, "A" & "B" from CROIX MOLIGNEAUX joining in route. The Battalion arrived at GERMAINE at 12:30pm and billeted there. 2/Lt HUTCHINSON A.M. appointed Intelligence Officer. Casualties Nil	67
GERMAINE	16ᵗʰ		Company training and bathing. Capt BOWMAN A.H. evacuated to hospital sick. Casualties nil	nil
"	17ᵗʰ		Company training. 2/Lt JORDAN R. admitted to hospital sick. Casualties nil. The Divisional Commander Maj General Colin MacKenzie C.B. presented medal ribbons and parchments. The recipients were:— Capt MANUEL J. (R.A.M.C. attached) Military Cross. 2/Lt BEAMAN R.A. 201463 Pte L. Rahman \ 201712 79 Sgt Mapp 201632 L/Cpl Yr. Davis	201973 Sgt. Harry Paramor \ Military Medal 203336 Pte J.H. Seaton / 201316 Pte H.H. Jones 201047 Sgt J. Stanute \ 203534 Sgt Johnson 201454 L/Cpl Chilton Divisional Commanders Parchment. In the evening the battalion relieved 2/6 Bat R. War. Regt in the right subsection of the right sector of the Divisional front ST QUENTIN. Relief completed without incident by 10:30 p.m. Casualties Nil.	6, 7₀

www.ingramcontent.com/pod-product-compliance
Lightning Source LLC
Chambersburg PA
CBHW081431160426
43193CB00013B/2246